"For some time now Michael Lebowitz has been patiently and provocatively remaking our conception of Marx's *Capital* and the potential for human development. In standing against a 'one-sided' reading of Marx for an insistence on seeing workers struggling to make their own world, Lebowitz has pushed to the side stale, top-down theses of social transformation through statist planning set apart from workers' organization and participation. Indeed, in his essential new book it is the building of workers' capacities and communities that transforms circumstances and contexts in a process of contested reproduction against capital. This is a directive to think of community not as a romanticized place standing against the storms of an outside world, but community as a process of struggle to meet and self-govern over common needs against the ceaseless demands of accumulation, alienated work, and the vandalism of the earth. Could any text be more important to read, discuss, and debate in the harsh times we face today?"**—GREG ALBO**, Professor of Political Economy, York University; coeditor, *The Socialist Register*

"Michael Lebowitz is certainly no faithful disciple of Marx. But he can claim to incarnate the best type of 'Marxist' that we need to break the circle of the capitalist rush to the destruction of the planet and the post-socialist ideological paralysis: resuming the critique of the economy at the point of Ricardo's default, where Marx himself had backed, and pushing the dialectical idea of 'contested reproduction' to the lively conflict of the two histories that inhabit our world and our lives. A book as clear and straightforward as it is radical."**—ETIENNE BALIBAR**, coauthor, *Reading Capital*

"This book should be mandatory for all economics, political science, and social philosophy classes. Comrades—especially younger ones—will find it immensely helpful for years to come. The sweep of the work is truly impressive; comprehensive and clear on everything essential for understanding the horrors of capitalism and the paths toward a better world."**—TONY SMITH**, Professor of Philosophy and Political Science, Iowa State University

"In twelve concisely and clearly written chapters, Lebowitz, among the best radical economists in the world, shows that in *Capital*, Marx failed to fully appreciate that the accumulation of capital results in two products—commodities of all kinds and the workers themselves. The latter, the 'second product' of capitalist production, is shaped by capital so that the working class is both badly divided and not fully cognizant of an all-encompassing alienation. Equally missing from *Capital* is a full grasp of how the collective actions of workers not only improve their life circumstances but also radically change them, preparing them to become society's eventual protagonists, those who will abolish capitalism and create the collective commonwealth, which alone can overcome the multiple crises that now confront us, especially ecological disaster."—**MICHAEL D. YATES**, author, *Can the Working Class Change the World?*

"In this admirable and timely book, Michael Lebowitz deepens and extends the understanding of capitalism that he developed in his prize-winning *Beyond Capital*. He argues persuasively that building critically on Marx's conceptualisation of capitalism as an organic system is indispensable to diagnosing the ills of the contemporary world—in particular the growing 'crisis of the Earth System' that threatens to overwhelm us."—**ALEX CALLINICOS**, former Professor of European Studies, King's College London

"In this insightful contribution, Michael Lebowitz continues to rigorously demonstrate the one sidedness of Marx's understanding of capitalism in *Capital* and shifts Marxism, as a dialectical and systems view of the world, to new ground. It is essential reading to understand the importance of solidarity in these times of senile and catastrophic capitalism."—**VISHWAS SATGAR**, Principal Investigator Emancipatory Futures Studies; Editor of the Democratic Marxism series, University of the Witwatersrand, South Africa

"This book is a provocation, as much for traditional Marxists as for the various schools of nontraditional Marxism. It puts the question on the table of whether Marx's *Capital* could be an obstacle for understanding class struggle and revolutionary practice. Michael Lebowitz questions what is taken for granted by the majority of Marxists. He draws conclusions from this critique, which also influences the offered vision of a non-capitalist future."
—**MICHAEL HEINRICH**, author, *Karl Marx and the Birth of Modern Society*

BETWEEN
CAPITALISM AND COMMUNITY

MICHAEL A. LEBOWITZ

MONTHLY REVIEW PRESS

New York

Library of Congress Cataloging-in-Publication Data
available from the publisher

ISBN paper 978-1-58367-886-2
ISBN cloth 978-1-58367-887-9

Typeset in Minion Pro and Brown

MONTHLY REVIEW PRESS, NEW YORK
monthlyreview.org

5 4 3 2 1

Contents

Preface | 7

Introduction: Class Struggle and *Capital* | 11

PART I. IN PRAISE OF DIALECTICS | 17

1. The Atomism of Neoclassical Economics | 19

2. The Truth Is the Whole | 29

PART II. ONE-SIDED MARXISM | 41

3. Marx's Conceptualization of Capitalism as an Organic System | 43

4. Crises and Non-Reproduction | 54

PART III. THE SECOND PRODUCT | 71

5. Never Forget the Second Product | 73

6. The Burden of Classical Political Economy | 84

7. Capital's Need to Separate Workers | 96

PART IV. CONTESTED REPRODUCTION | 109

8. Beyond Atomism | 111

9. Between Organic Systems | 123

10. How to Find a Path to Community | 137

11. Taking a Path to Community | 150

12. The Political Instrument we Need | 161

Notes | 180

Index | 199

There are those that struggle all of their life.
They are the indispensable ones.
— Bertold Brecht, "In Praise of the Fighters"

For Marta Harnecker (1937–2019)
Popular Educator. Indispensable.

Preface

I am not a disciple of Marx. My goal is not to prove that Marx was right. This, Marx knew, is how a theory disintegrates. Commenting upon the disciples of Hegel and Ricardo, he argued that disintegration of a theory begins when the point of departure is "no longer reality, but the new theoretical form in which the master had sublimated it" and, accordingly, when the disciples are driven to "explain away" the "often paradoxical relationship of this theory to reality."[1] Unfortunately, Marx's disciples often have embraced the Two Whatevers: "Whatever is in *Capital* is right, whatever is not in *Capital* is wrong."

But the problem is not only what disciples do. Marx understood that the master, for whom "the science was not something received, but something in the process of becoming," may "fall into one or another apparent inconsistency through some sort of accommodation." And this, I demonstrate, is precisely what occurred in *Capital*—an accommodation that produced theoretical blindness.

Why does this matter? It matters if theoretical deficiencies hinder what must be our goal, which is to end this destructive system of capitalism and to replace it with a new society based upon communality and solidarity. It matters if *Capital* obscured capital's "immanent drive" and "constant tendency" to divide the working class. It matters if the centrality of revolutionary practice, that simultaneous changing of circumstance and self-change that promotes the development of the capacities of the working class, plays no apparent role in *Capital*. It matters, in short, if we are to know how capitalism continues and what can bring it to an end.

Between Capitalism and Community continues my exploration of the continent that Marx discovered, a journey that began in 1982 with an article, "The One-Sidedness of Capital," which was followed by *Beyond Capital: Marx's Political Economy of the Working Class* (1992, 2003).[2] At the time, considering the logic of Marx's discussion of capital, I attributed problems in *Capital* to the absence of the book on Wage-Labor that he originally intended to write as part of his Economics.[3]

Between Capitalism and Community begins not with the logic of capital but by considering the relation between a whole and its parts. From this dialectical perspective, our critique is deeper. We conclude that Marx's intellectual construct of capitalism as an organic system, a system of reproduction that produces its own premises, neither represents the logic of capital correctly nor reveals those elements in the concrete whole of capitalism that point to a different organic system, that of community.

Indeed, two diametrically opposed systems, capitalism and community, coexist and interpenetrate in a process of contested reproduction. The central question for revolutionaries, then, is how to create the conditions in which the elements of capitalism can be subordinated by the system of community, a matter that has become urgent as the result of the crisis of the Earth system.

Two themes I have raised in previous books (*Build It Now, The Socialist Alternative,* and *The Socialist Imperative*) are the necessity for a vision for the future and for a revolutionary party.[4] New in *Between Capitalism and Community* is that (a) the vision offered here is based explicitly upon the concept of the organic system of community, a system that produces its own premises; and (b) it is precisely the deformation of the elements of community within this process of contested reproduction that underlies the necessity for a revolutionary party.

What kind of party? This is not arbitrary, and it is definitely not the disciplined vanguard party (or sect) that purports to change circumstances for people. Grasping the centrality of revolutionary practice, the party that can go beyond capitalism, self-interest, and hierarchy to develop relations of community is one that stresses protagonism and the development of the capacities of people through all their activities. Rather than those who know, delivering their distilled knowledge to those who do not know, this is a political instrument that listens and learns. In this, I share the insistence of Marta Harnecker on the profoundly democratic nature of the necessary political instrument.[5]

I am happy to be working again with Michael Yates of Monthly Review Press because my experience with him on previous books has been all that I could hope for in an editor. Sadly, though, due to her extended battle against cancer and her death on 14 June 2019, I have not been able to complete this part of the journey with Marta, my comrade and partner. We have all lost one of the "indispensables" who struggle all their lives to build a better world. In completing this book, I miss not only her loving presence but also her wisdom in commenting upon my work. If this book does not suffer significantly as a result, it is because of all that I have already learned from her.

—27 FEBRUARY 2020

INTRODUCTION

Class Struggle and *Capital*

In *Beyond* Capital: *Marx's Political Economy of the Working Class*, I argued that there is a fundamental problem in *Capital*—its one-sidedness. Missing from *Capital* is the side of the workers themselves; absent is the struggle for the "worker's own need for development," and precisely because this is missing from *Capital*, so too is the revolutionary side.[1]

I noted that I was not alone in making this argument. In his *Poverty of Theory*, for example, E. P. Thompson described *Capital* as "a study of the logic of capital, not of capitalism, and the social and political dimensions of the history, the wrath and the understanding of the class struggle arising from a region independent of the closed system of economic logic."[2] Missing from *Capital*, he argued, are "men and women [who], in determinate productive relations, identify their antagonistic interests, and come to struggle, to think, and to value in class ways: thus the process of class formation is a process of self-making, although under conditions which are 'given.'"[3] Missing, in short, is real class struggle.

Similarly, Cornelius Castoriadis proposed that class struggle is outside the bounds of *Capital*. Marx presented, he argued, only capital's side of the struggle within production there, "letting the worker appear as a purely passive object of this activity." Whereas Castoriadis situated the problem of *Capital* in Marx's treatment of labor-power as a commodity (the faulty "cornerstone" that meant *Capital* was "built on sand"), for Thompson the problem was that Marx proceeded from Political Economy to "*capitalism . . . that is, the whole society, conceived as an 'organic system'*"; he was "sucked into a theoretical whirlpool," and the result was "not the overthrow of 'Political Economy' but *another* 'Political Economy.'"[4]

From the time of the *Grundrisse*, Thompson insisted, "the postulates ceased to be the self-interest of man and became the logic and forms of capital." And part of this "system of *closure*," in which all is subsumed within the circuits of capital where capital posits itself as an "organic system," is that capital's "self-development is determined by the innate logic inherent within the category." In this conception, "capital has become Idea, which unfolds itself in history." In the *Grundrisse*, Thompson declares, "Not once or twice, but in the whole mode of presentation—we have examples of *unreconstructed* Hegelianism."[5]

While I agreed that *Capital* lacked class struggle—or, more accurately, class struggle from the side of the worker—I insisted in *Beyond Capital* that the problem was not that capitalism was introduced as an organic system but rather that it was *not* one. Characteristic of an organic system, I argued, is that it produces all its necessary premises. However, while demonstrating that the reproduction of capital has as its necessary condition the reproduction of the working class, Marx left the latter to "the worker's drives for self-preservation and propagation."[6] Accordingly, I proposed that the system we observe in *Capital* was "*incomplete—incomplete at the very point that the reproduction of capital is revealed to require something outside of capital.*"[7]

Outside the system was the side of the worker, the side where workers struggle for their own goals, the side propelled by "the worker's own need for development." This, and not a "closed system of economic logic," was the reason for the exclusion of "history, the wrath and the understanding of the class struggle" from *Capital*.[8] Indeed, unless we incorporate that missing side (and, thus, two-sided class struggle), *Beyond* Capital concluded that our concept of capitalism is infected.

Two basic arguments have been marshalled against this critique. In one, the introduction of class struggle into *Capital* is declared to be premature; in another, we are told that class struggle is already present in the theory of *Capital*. Arguing the former position, a follower of the Japanese Uno School in his review of *Beyond* Capital insisted that discussion of class struggle belongs not "at the level of the theory of capital's inner logic" but at a later level of "stages" where matters of contingency and complexity are appropriately addressed.

Class struggle is banned from *Capital* in this particular argument because the unique Unoist distillation of *Capital* is "the theory of a purely capitalist society," a general equilibrium model in which the market mechanism (the law of value) ensures the reproduction of capitalism as a "self-perpetuating entity." From this perspective, Robert Albritton's dismissal of my argument as "old simplistic humanism" and "class struggle functionalism" is appropriate because class struggle is incompatible with this neoclassical reading of *Capital*. Indeed, rather than a class struggle perspective, Unoism offers "*unreconstructed* Hegelianism." As Tom Sekine, one of the guiding theorists of Unoism, declared: "The exact correspondence between the dialectic of capital and Hegel's *Logic* can scarcely be doubted."[9]

The argument that exploration of class struggle is premature, however, is not limited to this unique reading of *Capital*. Rejecting my introduction of the concept of the "degree of separation of workers," a variable meant to reflect the relative strength of the respective parties in struggle, Ben Fine insisted that "both the elements and incidence of class struggle are too varied, numerous and complex (multi-layered and impure)" to allow for the use of such a concept.[10] Precisely because the structures and processes leading from developments in the sphere of production to division of output are so many and complex, he argued that it was (and is) appropriate to put off the question of class struggle. "The incorporation of class struggle as a determinant," Fine proposed, "presumes a structure and complexity of analysis that goes far beyond that contained in Volume 1 of

Capital. No wonder, then, that the theory of wages is put off until a later volume or so of *Capital.*"[11]

Class struggle in this view relates to distribution, and, before distribution can be considered, we must understand the production of surplus value which "sets the parameters within which class struggle can be located." Indeed, for Fine, "The structures and processes of accumulation have to be specified before the mode, nature and impact of class struggle can be assessed."[12] Accordingly, given how "varied, numerous and complex" are the elements relating to class struggle, Fine concludes that I have been *premature* in insisting that class struggle be considered sooner: "The degree of separation simply leapfrogs from the abstract to the concrete."[13]

There are two central problems in Fine's argument.[14] One is that the variety, differentiation, and complexity he identifies at the level of the concrete applies as well to the standard of necessity, the length and intensity of the workday, and the level of productivity, all concepts essential for developing the concept of surplus value. Contrary to Fine, the existence of real complexity offers no special impediment to the introduction of the concept of the degree of separation at the level of *Capital.*

More significant, however, is Fine's premise that class struggle relates to distribution and not to the production of surplus value; that is, it occurs *post festum.* For this premise to hold, class struggle must be demonstrated to play no role in the determination of the workday, the standard of necessity, and the level of productivity. But this is precisely the begged question. Unless class struggle is irrelevant to the determination of the production of surplus value, then Fine's argument has no substance. Yet, as should be obvious from chapter 10 of *Capital,* Marx was unequivocal in insisting that class struggle determines the normal workday and thus is central to the production of surplus value.

Ironically, Marx's discussion of the struggle over the workday provides the basis for a different critique of my argument. Contrary to "those who argue that there is no class struggle in *Capital,*" Alex Callinicos proposes, "Chapter 10 is about class struggle." Indeed, he declares that "the chapter on the working day is the clearest refutation of the claim put forward, for example, by Michael Lebowitz, that '*Capital* is one-sided precisely because the worker is not present as the subject who acts herself against capital.'"[15]

The point of chapter 10, though, was not to introduce the worker as subject; rather, its focus was to emphasize capital's drive to extend the workday in search of absolute surplus value, a drive that physically and mentally destroys workers and threatens the reproduction of the working class. Indeed, the "voracious appetite" of capital is so destructive, Marx declares, that "the same necessity as forced the manuring of English fields with guano" brings forth state laws to place limits on capital's drive. Summarizing his historical account of capital's efforts to go beyond all limits to the workday, Marx noted that "capital therefore takes no account of the health and length of life of the worker, unless society forces it to do so."[16]

Certainly, the workers immediately affected by capital's effort to grow in this manner were an essential (although not the only) part of society's opposition to this assault. Yes, of course, Callinicos is right: Chapter 10 definitely introduces class struggle by workers. "Suddenly," Marx announces, "there arises the voice of the worker, which had previously been stifled in the sound and fury of the production process." And, suddenly, we do see that, in addition to the right of the capitalist, there is also the right of the worker, and that "between equal rights, force decides."[17]

In chapter 10, Marx described how English workers developed as a class in their struggles against capital's drive for absolute surplus value. We see there "the daily more threatening advance of the working-class movement," how workers moved from "passive, though inflexible and unceasing" resistance to begin open class protest; we see their growing "power of attack" and how a "long class struggle" shaped the new factory legislation. Indeed, Marx concluded that "the establishment of a normal workday is therefore the product of a protracted and more or less concealed civil war between the capitalist class and the working class."[18]

So, what then happens with that working-class subject in *Capital*?

Gone! That voice of the worker, that right of the worker, that civil war from the side of the worker suddenly *disappears*. Those working-class subjects who struggle against capital enter left onto the stage in chapter 10, but their bodies are snatched, and they are replaced in *Capital* (as we will see) by workers who look upon the requirements of capital as "self-evident natural laws," workers who guarantee "in perpetuity" the reproduction of capital.

Yes, there is that struggle over the workday, but why didn't the absence of *wage struggles* in *Capital* sound an alarm bell? We know, as Callinicos does, that Marx was well aware of the struggles at the time of the working class over wages. Indeed, Callinicos cites *Value, Price and Profit* from this period, indicating that Marx stressed that "the working man constantly presses in the opposite direction" to the capitalist over wages. Callinicos describes that work (rather than *Capital*) as Marx's "most developed discussion of the strictly economic struggle." Accordingly, doesn't Callinicos's proposal that this discussion "may be seen as a complement" to *Capital* weaken his claim that the worker is present in *Capital* as the subject who struggles for herself against capital?[19]

If workers as subjects indeed did disappear from *Capital* after chapter 10, did that reimposed silence have any implications with respect to our understanding of the logic of capital? And was chapter 10 the result of a lapse on Marx's part or did class struggle on the part of workers not belong there? That is, as Albritton and Fine might suggest, did chapter 10 introduce an alien element into *Capital*?

When we investigate the concept of capitalism as an organic system, it returns us to these various critiques, especially that of Thompson, and opens up questions that I did not pose before. In particular, revisiting my earlier point about the one-sidedness of *Capital* is like pulling on a loose thread and causing much to unravel, not the least of which are the arguments of many Marxist theorists.

PART I

IN PRAISE OF
DIALECTICS

1

The Atomism of Neoclassical Economics

How can we understand capitalism? Neoclassical economics, which is to say, mainstream economics, rarely uses the name. Rather, it talks about the "market system" or the free market, a system in which individual property owners (both those who own material resources and those who own merely their personal capacities) contract with each other in their self-interest. And, as long as they are free to contract and free to choose, we are assured that the result gives us the best of all possible worlds.[1]

Neoclassical economics begins (and ends) with the individual. And this individual is treated as an isolated individual atom: the isolated individual consumer, the isolated individual capitalist owner, the isolated worker. Further, this individual is assumed to be rational, which the theory equates with self-interested. So, as a rational individual, this person is always looking to maximize self-interest, that is, to maximize profits or wages or the utility obtained from the goods purchased. If not doing that, then by definition the individual is not rational. In short, this individual always searches for the right point, the optimum point, in his or her self-interest. Thorstein Veblen, at the beginning of the twentieth century, described this as the view of the individual as "a lightning calculator of pleasures and pains."[2]

And that's a very accurate picture of the starting point of this theory, which is the idea of the individual as a calculator or, better yet, as a computer. Certain information is fed into this computer: what it wants to maximize, the resources at its disposal, the technologies that are relevant, and the prices of things. And, on the basis of this information, the computer turns out the correct solution, namely the one that maximizes pleasure or minimizes pain. So, for example, the computer, if a consumer, will decide how much it will purchase of different products based upon the relative utility it receives from each product and their relative prices. Pleasure versus pain.

Or the computer, if a worker, will decide how much it wants to work based on its preferences for leisure versus work and the wage (or alternative sources of income like welfare payments). And the computer, if it is a capitalist, will determine whether to use a machine or worker based on the relative prices of each and the nature of the technology—and whether to use a skilled or unskilled worker based upon the relative price and the relative efficiency of each, given the technology. Or the computer may be a criminal. As a rational criminal, this computer considers the benefits and costs of various acts and chooses those crimes for which the benefits are highest and the costs (the likelihood of being caught and the extent of punishment) are least. Or the computer will determine the best possible characteristics of a potential spouse, weighing pleasure and pain.

It's all about rational choice. In each case, the computer will generate a correct solution given the data. It will choose the optimum point that maximizes pleasure relative to pain or minimizes pain relative to pleasure. That's the starting point and premise of neoclassical economics—that the individual will be rational and will choose the best solution possible in his self-interest. As Veblen put it, the individual is presumed to be "in stable equilibrium except for the buffets of the impinging forces that displace him in one direction or another."

Now, the neoclassical economist doesn't care what equilibrium the computer has generated. What interests the neoclassical economist is how the computer solution will change if one piece of data is changed. It is obvious that if you change the data fed into that computer, it will generate a different optimum solution. So, that is the principal question neoclassical economists pose: let us change the value of one variable and see what the new equilibrium will be. Significantly, neoclassical economists do not pose this as a process that occurs in real time. Rather, they just want to change one variable and to see what the lightning calculator of pleasure and pain would do. But this is not a process that occurs in time. Because in a *real* world if we did change variable X, this could affect variable Y, and a change in variable Y might affect variable Z or variable X itself (in other words, create a feedback process). In real time, there are always processes of interaction, but neoclassical economics is not considering a real process that occurs in real time. That is why the critical phrase used is "all other things equal" (or, in Latin, *ceteris paribus*). We change one bit of data and nothing else.

So, with that in mind, let's think like a neoclassical economist. What happens if we raise the price of one consumer product? Well, obviously that increases the pain of purchasing that product, so the computer as consumer will generate a result in which less of that product is purchased and more of another. A new optimum solution is generated by the computer. Or let us raise the wage. The computer as capitalist, in comparison to the original situation, would choose to use a machine rather than a worker because the pain of hiring the worker has increased. Or let's increase payments for welfare. The computer as worker chooses to go on welfare rather than to get a job. It's all very simple. In every case, the question asked by neoclassical economic theory is what that individual, the instantaneous calculator of pleasure and pain, will choose in the second case compared to the first case. And the answer is self-evident. Given that the individual is an instantaneous calculator of pleasure and pain, he would make a different decision. If a potential particular pain is increased, choose less; if a potential particular pleasure is increased, choose more.

In fact, the answer is so self-evident that it is not necessary to derive the answer from any evidence. All the economists have to do is engage in a process of deduction: self-examination, self-interrogation. They ask, what would *I* do under the circumstances? Now, the economists know that they are rational. In other words, they know that rational persons like themselves act out of self-interest and only that. Indeed, neoclassical economists are particularly rational in this sense; that is, people who study neoclassical economics tend to be much more self-oriented and selfish than people who study in other fields.

Here, then, you have the basic wisdom of neoclassical economics, which serves as the basis and justification for neoliberal state policies. For example, if there's unemployment insurance and the benefits are increased, the logical conclusion of neoclassical economics is that you'll get more people who choose unemployment. So, the neoclassical economist says, "unemployment insurance causes unemployment." The same economists also tell us that having programs in support of single mothers causes mothers to be single and need support. Or they'll tell us that having welfare payments based on the number of children in a family—that is, the larger the number of children, the larger the payment—leads to increases in the number of children on welfare. In other words, increase the benefits and more people will choose to be single mothers on welfare. Or if you reduce the cost to individuals of healthcare and the cost of visits to doctors, people will go to the doctors and use hospitals more and the result will be significant increases in the cost of providing healthcare. Therefore, it is simple neoclassical economics that the way to reduce the cost of healthcare is by charging more for it. Clearly, the rational individual under these circumstances will choose health over sickness. Or they'll tell us that if you raise the minimum wage, capitalists will hire fewer workers; so, raising the minimum wage produces unemployment. The thinking is pervasive. A neoclassical economist will tell you that seatbelt legislation is bad because, by reducing the risk of serious injury, more people will drive recklessly; thus,, seatbelt legislation causes accidents.

Look at the policies that flow from neoclassical economics. Do you want to increase employment? Lower wages, reduce welfare payments, and reduce taxes on capital so it invests more? Do you want to lower the number of children growing up dependent upon welfare?

Lower the payments to welfare mothers. Do you want to reduce the cost of healthcare? Increase the charge for healthcare. And, most of all, if you want *anything* good, reduce the interference of the state in the economy—except, and this tells us something about the real beliefs of the economists, the role of the police and the judiciary in enforcing property rights.

Certainly, you don't try to solve the problem of poverty through state programs. For neoclassical economists, the way to solve poverty is by removing the state and letting the market work. And it's by individuals making the right choices, for example, by investing in their education (beginning around age six, one economist said in a seminar at my university). If you try to help the poor, that will reduce their incentive. And it is not appropriate to engage in redistribution of income and wealth by taxing the rich to support the poor; this will lead both the rich and the poor to reduce their incentive. A cartoon on my office door for many years described this theory well. One frame said, "The way to give the rich more incentive is to give them more money"; the other frame said, "The way to give the poor more incentive is to give them *less* money"!

The message is clear: leave everything to those rational individuals. When you try to "do good" through the state, you just make everything worse. Rent controls? Housing shortage. Price controls for food? Starvation. In the strange world of "all other things equal," by definition, there is only one answer: hands off, *laissez-faire*. And it is a strange world. Recall the proposition that unemployment insurance causes unemployment. The premise is that unemployment is the result of rational choice, that is, unemployment is *voluntary*. People are *choosing* not to have jobs. They just *look* like they're out of work involuntarily. They may even think so themselves, but neoclassical economists know better. Unemployment is voluntary. If people *wanted* to work, they could get jobs by working for lower wages. But what if you're a little skeptical and say, No, capitalists are firing and laying off workers! That doesn't look very voluntary on the part of the workers. One neoclassical economist responded by saying that the employer has *anticipated* the worker's choice. He anticipates that the worker would prefer to be fired than to work at a lower wage, and so the employer fires the worker "to the mutual satisfaction of both employee and employer."[3]

But how do we go from those isolated individual computers to talk about policy proposals at the level of a society? Well, those neoclassical economists just combine those computers, assuming that society is simply the sum of the isolated individuals within it. That's what society is for them, the place where those computers can interact. It is where those isolated self-interested individuals come together for their mutual benefit. And that's all society is! No one made this point better than former British prime minister Margaret Thatcher: "There's no such thing as *society*. There are individual men and women and there are families."

So that's what happens in society according to the neoclassical economist. We move from a single rational computer to two rational computers, each attempting to maximize its self-interest, and they engage in exchange; they can specialize in a certain kind of activity and exchange. Just start everyone off with an "initial endowment" and let the trading begin (quickly, before there are any questions about the inequality of those initial endowments!). Each person gets what he or she wants from the other by showing that it is to the other's advantage. As Adam Smith stated, "It is not from the benevolence of the butcher, the brewer or the baker that we expect our dinner, but from regard to their own interest." So each party to an exchange benefits or there wouldn't be an exchange.

Further, as long as people are free to engage in any exchange, they will be able to make the best possible exchange. For example, if a particular capitalist won't pay a worker what she is worth, the worker can go elsewhere. So the result is that in a free market everyone will get what each deserves. John Bates Clark, a leading U.S. economist early in the last century, said it all very explicitly. He began his book, *The Distribution of Wealth*, by announcing:

It is the purpose of this work to show that the distribution of the income of society is controlled by a natural law, and that this law, if it worked without friction, would give to every agent of production the amount of wealth which that agent creates.[4]

You get what you deserve. So don't complain. If you don't get very much, it's because you are not worth very much. But it is the best you can do.

The result of the combination of these rational, self-seeking individuals, thus, is that everyone benefits. This is what Adam Smith called the "Invisible Hand." It is the proposition that allows neoclassical economists to move from the rational individual to the rational society. It says, simply, that when an individual seeks his self-interest, he promotes the public good: "He is in this, as in many other cases, led by an invisible hand to promote an end which was no part of his intention." In other words, selfishness is good. Or, as Gordon Gecko said in Oliver Stone's classic movie *Wall Street*: "Greed is good."

Where did the invisible hand come from? For Adam Smith and many others at the time and after, the answer was clear: it came from God. A familiar view in the eighteenth century was that God created a world of economic harmony in which everyone benefits everyone else by following his own self-interest. That particular religious faith became economic faith, a secular religion, and a central part of that secular faith is that as long as there is no interference by the state, all will be well. As the U.S. economist John Kenneth Galbraith described this view, "In a state of bliss, there is no place for a Ministry of Bliss."[5]

Very simply, neoclassical economics is a justification of the existing society, with all of its inequality and injustice. Neoclassical economics serves as a justification of capitalism. But not because it talks about capitalism. Rather, that justification flows from its fundamental assumption that "if you can understand the smallest parts of the system in isolation from one another, then all you have to do is to put them together correctly in order to understand the whole."[6] Accordingly, since every unit acts rationally and maximizes self-interest, so also does society, the sum of the many ones. As Frédéric Bastiat, a nineteenth-century French economist, articulated this premise, "That which is right with regard to one person is also right with regard to society."[7] As long as all are free to choose, it is the best of all possible worlds.

True, there is a problem with the way neoclassical theory moves from the premise of a rational individual to the conclusion that the society is rational. As Keynes pointed out in a famous example, there is a significant fallacy in this inference. Any individual can decide to increase his savings and improve his future position. However, *all* individuals cannot. By lowering their consumption, they reduce aggregate spending and that leads to lower production, lower employment, and lower income for all. This is called the "paradox of thrift," and it is a classic example of the "fallacy of composition," the logical flaw in saying that what is true for one is necessarily true for all.

When people act as if the properties of the individual parts can be assumed to be the properties of the whole, the results can be quite different from their expectations. If one person stands up in a theater, he can see better. But if all people stand up? If one country devalues its currency, it can increase exports, reduce its imports and stimulate the economy. But if *all* countries devalue their currency? What happens if a country decides that it can be more competitive internationally by destroying trade unions and driving down the wages of workers? What happens if all competing countries do the same? One person goes to university in order to improve his chance at getting a job, but what if all people do? (Well, the answer is go to graduate school!) In this case, one writer commented, the value of your education depends not only on how much you have but also on how much the person ahead of you in the job line has.

In short, we can't just add up the individuals. Because they are *interdependent.* And interdependence is pervasive in the real world, as are its effects, which can be seen most obviously in the crisis of our common home, the earth. In its theory, though, given that it begins with each rational individual only taking into account the things he has to pay for, neoclassical economics has some difficulty explaining how the rational choices of individuals can lead to irrational social outcomes. So, to the extent that it can, it sweeps results of interdependency offstage into a category called "externalities." As it turns out, externalities are everywhere, and they are an anomaly for a theory that simply adds up individuals without taking into account their interdependence and interaction. So, the way neoclassical theorists deal with this in their work is by assuming that there *are* no interdependencies, no externalities, and if there are, they are trivial—minor, second-order effects that can be ignored without losing too much explanatory power. Unfortunately for the theory, this increasingly lacks any credibility, as we exist in a conjuncture marked by the crisis of the earth system.

By not beginning with the recognition of interdependence, neoclassical economics falsifies the nature of both parts and whole. Consider the following example of interdependency, which relates to the fallacy of composition. The idea comes from G. A. Cohen, a British Marxist philosopher, but I liked it so much I revised it and made it my own and introduced it in my first lectures for my Marxian economics class:[8]

On the floor of a locked room in which there are ten people, there is a single heavy key. Anyone can pick up the key, go to the door, unlock it, and leave. But once that happens, *no one else* can get out. So, the question Cohen posed is: Are these people *free*? Each individual is free to pick up the key and leave. But it is a fallacy of composition to conclude from this that *everyone* can leave. Their freedom is conditional; it depends upon no one else exercising their freedom. Whatever happens, there will be nine people trapped in the room. Cohen used this example to talk about what he called the "structural unfreedom of the proletariat," namely, how any worker could become a capitalist, but *all* workers couldn't become capitalists (a point that Marx had earlier made in one of his many examples of the fallacy of composition).

But why in this case is it wrong to assume that what is true of an individual is true for the whole group? *Because there is a constraint on the whole.* It is a structural constraint upon the whole that doesn't apply to any single individual. There is only one key. The particular interdependence of these people is given by the particular structure in which they exist, and their properties and characteristics flow from being parts of that particular whole. To describe and define those people accurately, they can't be viewed as isolated atoms, as individual computers that can be added up.

Can we talk about those individuals without first describing the society of which they are part? All we know about the individuals in the room at this point is that they are interdependent because of the external constraint. But surely there is more to say. We don't know the particular structure in which they exist, that is, the society of which they are part. Is this a society characterized by equality? Are these individuals separate and self-seeking or do they know and care for each other? If, for example, there is a limited quantity of water in this locked room, surely the nature of social relations among those individuals matters. Are they atomistic individuals free to take what they want or are they functioning as members of a community? How can we understand anything without beginning with the whole and the nature of relations within that whole?

This is one way Marxian political economy differs from neoclassical economics. Rather than starting with individuals and markets, it begins with the nature of the system, a whole characterized by particular relations among parts of that whole. In particular, *Capital*'s focus was upon exploring capitalism as a system, upon analyzing the logic of capital and the dynamic tendencies that flow from the properties of that system.

2

The Truth Is the Whole

By beginning from abstract individuals, neoclassical economics is one of the best examples of the "Cartesian reductionism" that Richard Levins and Richard Lewontin described in *The Dialectical Biologist*.[1] This reductionism, which is characteristic of the dominant approach in many sciences, "takes parts as given prior entities that can be defined in isolation and can have their properties considered in some ideal isolated prior state before these units become articulated into wholes."[2]

The alternative to this methodological perspective, Levins and Lewontin argue, is a dialectical worldview. "The truth is the whole," Hegel insisted in his *Phenomenology of Mind*, and several inferences flow from that dictum.[3] For one, we need to recognize that parts cannot be understood outside of the context of the particular whole in which they are part. Further, the whole as such must be understood as a particular combination of differing elements that mutually interact. Identifying these and the nature of their interaction allows us to explore the conditions for the reproduction of that whole or its transcendence.

Parts and Wholes

How can we understand the individuals in the locked room without examining the conditions in which they exist? For Marx, individuals are the ensemble of their social relations. Accordingly, rather than beginning with the particular interest of individuals, Marx insisted that the content of individual interest "as well as the form and means of its realization, is given by social conditions independent of all." In contrast to the doctrine of the economists that "each pursues his private interest and only his private interest; and thereby serves the private interests of all, the general interest, without willing or knowing it," Marx declared that we need to begin with the whole, because "private interest is itself already a socially determined interest, which can be achieved only within the conditions laid down by society and with the means provided by society."[4]

This emphasis upon the priority of the whole, philosopher György Lukács argued, was central to Marx's dialectical perspective: "The category of totality, the all-pervasive supremacy of the whole over the parts, is the essence of the method which Marx took over from Hegel and brilliantly transformed into the foundations of a wholly new science."[5]

The concept of totality allows us to reject the premise that parts have "intrinsic properties, which they possess in isolation and which they lend to the whole." By learning to think dialectically, we can see that parts "acquire properties by virtue of being parts of a particular whole, properties they do not have in isolation or as parts of another whole"; we understand that the particular properties of parts only "come into existence in the interaction that makes the whole."[6] Interaction, the whole, makes the part.

Connect, connect! That is Marx and all dialectical thinkers! For Lenin, the "necessity of connection" was central to a dialectical perspective. Reading Hegel's *Science of Logic*, he declared: "The basic idea is one of genius: that of the universal, allsided, *vital* connection of everything with everything." As Marx did before him, Lenin learned from Hegel the need to grasp "the all-sidedness and all-embracing character of the interconnection of the world":

A river and the *drops* in this river. The position of *every* drop, its relation to the others; its connection with the others; the direction of its movement; its speed; the line of the movement—straight, curved, circular, etc.—upwards, downwards. The sum of the movement. . . . There you have *à peu près* [approximately] the picture of the world according to Hegel's *Logic*—of course minus God and the Absolute.[7]

In contrast to beginning with this explicit recognition of the "connection of everything with everything," in the Cartesian reductionism identified by Levins and Lewontin, the parts spring fully grown from the forehead of the analyst and "come together to make wholes." In sum, the difference between the reductionist and dialectical perspectives was described well by philosopher Bertell Ollman:

> Unlike non-dialectical research, where one starts with some small part and through establishing its connections to other such parts tries to reconstruct the larger whole, dialectical research begins with the whole, the system, or as much of it as one understands, and then proceeds to an examination of the part to see where it fits and how it functions, leading eventually to a fuller understanding of the whole from which one has begun.[8]

Of course, the reductionist perspective understands that we must talk about the whole and that parts interact. Further, in its more sophisticated variants (such as systems theory), it recognizes that those interactions produce effects such that the whole is more than the sum of its parts taken individually. But what are those parts that are interacting and what is the effect of that interaction? Levins and Lewontin argue that even the more sophisticated and large-scale versions of reductionism take as their "elements unitary variables that are the 'atoms' of the system, prior to it, and qualitatively unchanging as they ebb and flow." The variables increase and decrease as the result of their interaction. "But the wholes are not allowed to transform the parts, except quantitatively."[9]

Here, then, is the essential error of all reductionism: those given fixed parts, which are the starting point, may be combined, may coexist, may even interact—but they are not understood to *interpenetrate*! Once you acknowledge interpenetration and thus transformation of the parts in their interaction, you can no longer treat the parts as fixed and independent. Parts make wholes but also wholes make parts. In short, the relation of parts is "not mere 'interconnection' or 'interaction' but a deeper interpenetration that transforms them so that the 'same' variable may have a very different significance in different contexts and the behavior of the system can alter its structure."[10]

If interpenetration is central to a Marxian dialectical view, then we must accept that the same particular part (for example, commodity exchange) in two systems does not mean that the systems are identical or, indeed, that the properties of the parts themselves are identical in these different wholes. Interpenetration means that parts are always determined by the whole, that they are transformed qualitatively in their interactions. "The category of totality, the all-pervasive supremacy of the whole over the parts," as Lukács understood, is the "essence" of dialectics.

The First Question: Reproduction

If the whole is not the sum of its isolated parts, what is the truth of the whole? Lenin's response was: "The *totality of all* sides of the phenomenon, of reality and their reciprocal *relations*—that is what truth is composed of."[11] Reciprocal relations, however, are not passive relations; rather, reciprocal interaction is the process described by Levins and Lewontin in which "elements recreate each other by interacting and are recreated by the wholes of which they are parts." A central dialectical principle, accordingly, is that "change is a characteristic of all systems and all aspects of all systems."[12]

The truth of the whole, in short, is constant movement and change as the result of the interaction of the elements it contains. Whereas "non-dialectical thinkers in every discipline," Ollman comments, "are involved in a nonstop search for the 'outside agitator,' for something or someone that comes from outside the problem under examination and is the cause for whatever occurs," a dialectical thinker focuses upon what is internal to the whole.[13] As Marx put it, "mutual interaction takes place between the different moments. This [is] the case with every organic whole."[14]

From this perspective, change and development cannot be viewed as a simple relationship of cause and effect, of constants and variables, of independent and dependent variables. For example, cause becomes effect, effect becomes cause in this reciprocal interaction. As Lenin noted in his reading of Hegel, causality "is only a small particle of universal interconnection"; indeed, "the all-sidedness and all-embracing character of the interconnection of the world . . . is only one-sidedly, fragmentarily and incompletely expressed by causality."[15] Engels made the same point in a response to critics:

> What all these gentlemen lack is dialectics. All they ever see is cause on the one hand and effect on the other. But what they fail to see is that this is an empty abstraction, that in the real world such metaphysically polar opposites exist only in a crisis, that instead the whole great process takes place solely and entirely in the form of interplay. . . . So far as they are concerned, Hegel might never have existed.[16]

Precisely because of the constant interaction of its internal relations, there is movement and self-movement within the whole, "*internally-necessary* movement." This was the point made by Hegel that Lenin quoted and emphasized: "Contradiction is the *root of all movement and vitality,* and it is only insofar as it contains a Contradiction that anything *moves and has impulse and activity.*"[17] And yet, this emphasis upon constant change raises a central question: How is it that things do persist?

The first question of two that "Marxism encourages me to ask," Richard Levins notes, is "why are things the way they are instead of a little bit different?" The non-dialectical answer is that "things are the way they are because nothing much is happening to them." It is the belief that "stasis is the normal state of affairs, and change must be accounted for." In contrast, "A dialectical view begins from the opposite end: change is universal and much is happening to change everything. Therefore, equilibrium and stasis are special situations that have to be explained."[18]

The first question posed, in short, is "in the face of constantly displacing influences, how do things remain recognizably what they are?" The general answer offered as explanation is "homeostasis, the self-regulation observed in physiology, ecology, climatology, the economy and indeed all systems that show any persistence." While such system-stability is often modeled mathematically by starting from a set of variables that are prior entities with intrinsic properties, thus remaining "vulnerable to the reproach of being large-scale reductionism," Levins and Lewontin articulate a specific dialectical answer that we must keep before us: "Our answer is that things are the way they are because of the actions of opposing processes."[19]

Think about equilibrium and stasis in this context. "Homeostasis takes place," Levins and Lewontin indicate, "through the actions of positive and negative feedback loops. If an initial impact sets processes in motion that diminish that initial impact, we refer to it as negative feedback, whereas if the processes magnify the original change the feedback is positive."[20] As biologists, Levins and Lewontin draw upon many examples from the natural sciences to illustrate how negative feedback can negate initial changes, for example, how pesticides may increase pest population by killing off pest predators and how rapidly falling blood sugar produces anxiety that is relieved by rising glucose. However, their example of how rising food prices stimulate increased agricultural production, which tends in turn to lower food prices, indicates that the existence of negative feedback as a support for reproduction of an existing system is not limited to the natural world.[21] Negative feedback is present in all homeostasis and self-regulation, and the dialectical task is to explain why there is stability and equilibrium, how "things are the way they are because of the temporary balance of opposing forces."[22]

When the opposing forces contained within a system are balanced, then the system through its self-regulating processes produces and reproduces its own conditions of existence. However, the joint action of those opposing forces can be destabilizing rather than a basis for the reproduction of the system. When positive feedback exceeds negative feedback, when major changes occur (or even minor ones if the system is in stress), "the original system can no longer persist as it was. The system may go into wider and wider fluctuations and breakdown, or the parts themselves, which have meaning only within a particular whole, may lose their identity as parts and give rise to a qualitatively new system."[23]

Accordingly, the dialectical task is not only to understand the stasis and equilibrium of a system but also its opposite, that is, what can produce its instability. Whereas under normal conditions small events tend to be subsumed by the system's self-regulating processes, under "severe or unusual general stress conditions" a tiny event may produce major effects (as envisioned in the concept of the "butterfly effect"). The latter is possible, Levins and Lewontin note, "when a system is poised on the brink of a qualitative change." From this perspective, "the task of promoting change is one of promoting the conditions under which small, local events can precipitate the desired restructuring."[24]

Knowing the Whole

But how can we know the whole? Levins and Lewontin argue that we can't. "Despite Hegel's dictum that 'the truth is the whole,'" they explain, "we cannot study 'the whole.'" Nevertheless, they insist, Hegel's assertion has clear practical value. For one, understanding that the truth is the whole means that we should always try to extend the boundaries of the questions we are considering. Further, it directs us to admit that "after we have defined a system in the broadest terms we can at the time, there is always something more out there that might intrude to change our conclusions."[25] But given that the concept of the whole is implicit in their declaration (and obvious from their work), what does it mean to say that we cannot know the whole?

Consider the critical distinction Marx made in the Introduction to the *Grundrisse* between the concrete whole and its reproduction in the mind. While the real whole is "the point of departure for observation and conception," Marx insisted that mere observation and empirical study cannot possibly grasp the interconnections of that concrete totality. All that results from observation is a "chaotic conception of the whole."[26] Accordingly, if we are to understand the concrete totality, that "universal, all-sided, *vital* connection of everything with everything," then, as Lenin observed, we must develop concepts that "likewise must be hewn, treated, flexible, mobile, relative, mutually connected, united in opposites, in order to embrace the world."[27]

How did Marx grasp the interconnections of that concrete whole? In *Beyond* Capital: *Marx's Political Economy of the Working Class*, chapter 4, and in *Following Marx: Method, Critique and Crisis* (in particular chapters 5, 10, and 11), I offered an extended discussion of Marx's method.[28] I explained that Marx argued that we begin with the "simplest determinations" and concepts that are themselves the result of analysis of the concrete. Then we proceed on a step-by-step basis to deduce logically a conception of the whole "as a rich totality of many determinations and relations." This "method of rising from the abstract to the concrete," Marx stressed, is the "scientifically correct method"; it is "the way in which thought appropriates the concrete, reproduces it as the concrete in the mind." In short, this totality of thoughts is a product of "the working-up of observation and conception into concepts." It is "a product of a thinking head, which appropriates the world in the only way it can."[29]

That "thinking head" develops the connection between concepts by asking always (as Hegel did in his *Science of Logic*) the essential question: what does this concept imply, what is outside this concept but intimately connected to it? To the extent that a concept can be shown to imply a further concept, it demonstrates that it contains its negation, that it is not adequate in itself. Here is the "dialectical moment" that philosopher and sociologist Henri Lefebvre defined as the "expedient of the mind which finds itself obliged to move from a position it had hoped was definitive and to take account of something further."[30]

Armed by this dialectic of negativity, we can move to higher and richer concepts, each "enriched by the negation or opposite of the preceding concept."[31] Through this process, according to Hegel, "cognition rolls forward from content to content. This progress determines itself, first, in this manner, that it begins from simple determinatenesses and that each subsequent one is richer and more concrete." In this way, every step of the process is one of "dialectical progress [that] not only loses nothing and leaves nothing behind, but carries with it all that it has acquired, enriching and concentrating itself upon itself."[32]

A seemingly mystical adventure of concepts, but it is precisely how Marx proceeded in *Capital*. There, we follow Marx as he interrogates the commodity and discovers within it the concept of money. (These two concepts are inextricably linked and cannot be externally juxtaposed as the classical political economists did.) Considering the relationship of commodity and money, in which each is in turn mediator and end, we uncover the concept of capital in the sphere of circulation, and from here that of capital in the sphere of production, and then capital as a whole as a specific unity of production and circulation. Thus, an advance to ever richer and more concrete conceptions.[33]

As we might expect if we are thinking dialectically, our understanding of the parts changes as we advance in the direction of the "rich totality of many determinations and relations." The commodity, for example, looks different after development of the concepts of money, capitalist circulation, capitalist production, and capital as a whole. And the same is true of money and, indeed, capital itself. They must. Characteristic of dialectical reasoning, terms and moments are introduced in a one-sided manner, revealing their all-sidedness in the course of the construction of the totality. Only when we have successfully developed that "totality of thoughts" can we fully understand its elements.

But does that hour of our understanding ever come? Reading Hegel, Lenin remarked that truth should not be imagined "in the form of a bare picture"; rather, "the coincidence of thought with the object is a *process*." Indeed, he stressed, "cognition is the eternal, end-less approximation of thought to the object."[34] Absolutely central here is the distinction between the "real concrete" and the "concrete in the mind." We do not know the whole, if we mean by that the concrete totality. Rather, we have at any given point a more or less adequate mental reproduction of the concrete, a more or less useful intellectual construct.

As Ollman puts it, "Our knowledge of the real world is mediated through the construction of concepts in which to think about it; our contact with reality, insofar as we become aware of it, is contact with the conceptualized reality."[35] Whereas "the real concrete is simply the world in which we live, in all its complexity," we construct our under-standing of that world through a process of abstraction, which is "the intellectual activity of breaking this whole down into the mental units with which we think about it."[36]

Insofar as we acknowledge that we do not know the whole but at best can only endlessly approximate thought to the object, we must admit that our intellectual construct may misrepresent the real con-crete. Levins and Lewontin point to several possible reasons. One may be the particular abstractions through which we have attempted to reproduce the concrete in the mind:

> Different abstractions from the same wholes capture different aspects of the reality but also leave us with different blindnesses. Thus it is always necessary to recognize that our abstractions are intellectual constructs, that an "object" kicks and screams when it is abstracted from its context and may take its revenge in lead-ing us astray.[37]

But another potential problem may be premature closure, that is, we may not have sufficiently developed the concrete in the mind. Recognizing that only the whole is the truth, Levins and Lewontin insist that "we always have to be aware that there is more out there that might overwhelm our theories and thwart our best intentions."[38] What is excluded from our mental construct, indeed, may infect our concept of the whole and its parts. In particular, failing to incorporate new sides of categories under investigation and "seizing upon one side of a dichotomous pair or a contradiction as if it were the whole thing" can infect our concept of the whole with "one-sidedness."[39]

Finally, there may be a gap between the real whole and the mental construct by which we attempt to grasp the concrete because the concrete is not static and has *changed* in such a way as to invalidate our original concrete in the mind. As Levins and Lewontin argue, "We need a permanent awareness of the model as a human intellectual construct that is more or less useful within certain bounds and then can become nonsense."[40]

How, then, to proceed in studying capitalism? By building that intellectual construct, that concrete in the mind, which approximates the real concrete, and at the same time being open to the possibility that the concept of the whole that Marx developed in *Capital* was faulty and, indeed, one-sided. As Lukács insisted:

Orthodox Marxism . . . does not imply the uncritical acceptance of the results of Marx's investigations. It is not the "belief" in this or that thesis, nor the exegesis of a "sacred" book. On the contrary, orthodoxy refers exclusively to method.[41]

PART II

ONE-SIDED MARXISM

Marx's Conceptualization of Capitalism as an Organic System

What was the whole that Marx presented in *Capital*? Did that intellectual construct truly represent the real concrete, or was there "something else out there" that can infect our concept of the whole? To understand capitalism and the relation of its parts, Marx introduced the concept of capitalism as an organic system. This is a particular conception of the whole. In capitalism as an organic system ("the completed bourgeois system"), "every economic relation presupposes every other in its bourgeois economic form, and everything posited is thus also a presupposition; this is the case with every organic system."[1]

In short, all the elements within this organic system are parts that have been produced by the system; the completion of this system ("its development to its totality") "consists precisely in subordinating all elements of society to itself, or in creating out of it the organs which it still lacks. This is historically how it becomes a totality." Thus, in capitalism as an organic system, all the elements of capitalism have been successfully subordinated within the system.

Characteristic of "every organic system" is that the premises of the system are results that the system itself produces; this theme of the reproduction of premises permeates Marx's discussion in *Capital*.

For example, Marx pointed out that capital produces and reproduces material products and social relations, which are themselves presuppositions and premises of production. "Those conditions, like these relations, are on the one hand the presuppositions of the capitalist production process, on the other its results and creations; they are both produced and reproduced by it."[2] Similarly, considering the circuit of capital as a whole, Marx stressed that "all the premises of the process appear as its result, as premises produced by the process itself. Each moment appears as a point of departure, of transit, and of return." Indeed, all presuppositions, all preconditions, all premises are themselves results: "In a constantly revolving orbit, every point is simultaneously a starting point and a point of return."[3]

Production and reproduction of premises implies incessant renewal. As Marx opened his chapter on simple reproduction in Volume I of *Capital*:

> Whatever the social form of the production process, it has to be continuous, it must periodically repeat the same phases. A society can no more cease to produce than it can cease to consume. When viewed, therefore, as a connected whole, and in the constant flux of its incessant renewal, every social process of production is at the same time a process of reproduction.[4]

There you have the point that Marx wanted to stress—the necessity to recognize that capitalism is such a system of reproduction. "Capitalist production therefore reproduces in the course of its own process the separation between labour-power and the conditions of labour. It thereby reproduces and perpetuates the conditions under which the worker is exploited."[5] In this conception, capitalism is an organic system because it reproduces its premises—the capitalist and the wage-laborer:

> The capitalist process of production, therefore, seen as a total, connected process, i.e. a process of reproduction, produces not only commodities, not only surplus-value, but it also produces

and reproduces the capital-relation itself; on the one hand the capitalist, on the other the wage-labourer.[6]

Since capital and wage-labor, the premises of capitalist production, are "both produced and reproduced by it," to understand capitalism as a system we must look at precisely how the system is reproduced. We need to examine how it "creates its own presuppositions . . . by means of its own production process," how capital "no longer proceeds from presuppositions in order to become, but rather it is itself presupposed, and proceeds from itself to create the conditions of its maintenance and growth."[7]

Thinking about a system that is "itself presupposed" permits us to understand the nature of a system and why it persists; it explains "the structure of society in which all relations coexist simultaneously and support one another."[8] In short, by considering that "total, connected process" in incessant renewal, Marx was answering the first question of Levins and Lewontin—why things remain recognizably what they are.

The Second Question

A system in the process of developing upon the basis of presuppositions that it has *not* created itself, on the other hand, points to the second essential question that "Marxism encourages me to ask": How did things get the way they are? To this, Levins and Lewontin answer that "things are the way they are because they got that way, and not because they have to be that way, or always were that way, or because it's the only way to be." In short, in contrast to those necessary connections in an organic system, their answer to the question of "evolution, history and development" is *contingency*, the many possible routes to the development of a system that is presupposed and proceeds from itself.[9]

This separation between the two questions is precisely the one that Marx made in *Capital* by distinguishing between the reproduction of capitalist relations of production, on the one hand, and "so-called primitive accumulation of capital" on the other. Capitalist production presupposes, he insisted, the "capital-relation" (capital and wage-labor), that is, the "complete separation between the workers and the ownership of the conditions for the realization of their labour." In contrast, his discussion of original accumulation considers a particular example of how things "got that way," the historical process that "creates the capital-relation," namely, "the pre-history of capital, and of the mode of production corresponding to capital."[10]

With respect to the creation of the capital-relation, things indeed did get that way "not because they have to be that way, or always were that way, or because it's the only way to be." Enclosures, state regulation of wages, bloody colonial barbarism, and speculation in state debt were all elements that Marx described as part of that original creation of presuppositions for England and the Western European countries that followed that path. However, they were neither necessary in their particulars, nor were they part of the historic presuppositions of the capital-relation elsewhere (for example, in Japan).

This distinction between the reproduction of the system, on the one hand, and its original creation, on the other, makes it obvious why Marx first examined the conditions for the reproduction of the system rather than following the historical order, that is, the prehistory of capital. It demonstrates the serious error of proposing that Marx's discussion of original accumulation should be read first before grasping capitalism as an organic system. *If we don't know what the essential elements in capitalist relations of production are, how can we identify the critical historical events that contributed to create that system?* Only after Marx had revealed capital and wage-labor as the premises and results of capitalist production could he then focus upon the preconditions for the *initial* emergence of each. Theory, in short, guides the historical inquiry. Our method, Marx noted, "indicates the points where historical investigation must enter in"; understanding the nature of capitalism as an organic system "point[s] towards a past lying behind this system."[11]

What happens if you don't distinguish clearly between an organic system and a contingent set of historic presuppositions that create its starting point? By failing to distinguish between "historic premises," those "*past* presuppositions" that belong to the history of the formation of capital "but in no way to its *contemporary* history, i.e. not to the real system of the mode of production ruled by it," it is easy to obscure the specific nature of the system. That was Marx's point with respect to bourgeois economists who focused upon individual savings as the source of capital. By "formulating the conditions of its becoming as the conditions of its contemporary realization, i.e. presenting the moments in which the capitalist still appropriates as not-capitalist—because he is still becoming—as the very conditions in which he appropriates as *capitalist*," they were masking exploitation of workers as the condition of existence of capitalism.[12] In contrast, by considering capitalism as an organic system, as a system of reproduction, we understand that capital is the result of the exploitation of workers.[13]

Premises to Be Reproduced

"On the one hand the capitalist, on the other the wage-labourer." On the one hand, the owner of means of production and money who is focused upon the growth of his capital; on the other, the worker who lacks those means of production and accordingly must sell her ability to perform labor in order to purchase the means of subsistence. These, we see, are the specific premises of capitalist production, premises that must be reproduced in capitalism.

Capitalist and wage-laborer, however, presuppose other premises. Logically presupposed are commodity and money. Before capital can exploit wage-laborers in the process of production, it must be able to purchase labor-power as a commodity with money. The circuit of capital, in short, requires commodities, money, and labor-power as a commodity. Similarly, for the circuit of wage-labor, the worker must be able to take the money received as wages, and "it is the worker himself who converts the money into whatever use-values he desires; it is he who buys commodities as he wishes."[14] Thus, commodity and money are necessary premises for the circuits of capital and wage-labor.[15]

Naturally, commodity and money also have their premises. They imply a separation of producers such that their need for the products of each other is not satisfied through a direct social relation between the producers but, rather, only through a social relation between their products, a social relation expressed as the exchange value of their commodities. If the social relations among the producers were such as to permit a direct exchange of "activities, determined by communal needs and communal purposes," the conditions that require a commodity-money economy—that is, "the market"—would not be present; in short, atomization of the producers is a condition for commodity and money and thus capitalism.[16]

Further, for capitalist production and the exploitation of the wage-laborer to occur, a particular commodity must be available for the capitalist—labor-power as a commodity. And that, too, has its logical premise: the owner of money must find the free worker available on the commodity market, and that has a double condition: (1) as the owner of her labor-capacity, she is free to sell that capacity as a commodity, and (2) she is free of the means of production that would permit her to produce and sell commodities in which her labor has been objectified. Thus, the logical condition for the existence of labor-power as a commodity is that the worker is liberated from political constraints upon her person and is separated from the means of production.[17]

For capital to be reproduced, labor-power as a commodity must be reproduced. Having purchased use-values with his wages, the worker must be able to consume those (as well as private labor within the household).[18] "Now, as regards the worker's consumption," Marx commented, "this reproduces one thing, namely himself, as living labour capacity." Precisely, though, because this process of consumption is one that *annihilates* those use-values, it is a process that "simply reproduces the needy individual."[19] As a result, the worker must offer himself again as the seller of labor-power to the owner of money in order to obtain wages. Commodity and money in this respect are produced as labor-power and wages.

Capital as Premise

The reproduction of the side of capital requires two acts. Not only must the capitalist be able to compel the production of capital through the process of production, but he must be able to make that surplus value real through the process of circulation. The first act flows from the results of the worker's sale of his labor-power to the capitalist: "Firstly, the worker works under the control of the capitalist to whom his labour belongs," and "Secondly, the product is the property of the capitalist and not that of the worker, its immediate producer."[20] As the result of production within and through this particular set of property rights, the capitalist is able to compel the performance of surplus labor by workers and, as owner of the products of labor, that is, as the residual claimant, is the beneficiary of the surplus value they latently contain.

In the second act, however, reproduction of capital involves more than the existence of commodities containing the products of exploitation. In particular, "The capitalist must have contrived to sell his commodities, and to reconvert into capital the greater part of the money received from their sale."[21] In what Marx designated in Volume 2 of *Capital* as the third stage of the circuit of capital (after capital's appearance as buyer and as producer of commodities containing surplus value), "the capitalist returns to the market as seller." It is in Volume 2 that he explores what Volume 1 left "uninvestigated," the metamorphosis of capital through its different forms.[22] Here, we are shown the movement of capital from its commodity form to its money form through the sale of commodities and through which the surplus value latent in those commodities is made real (realized). Further, we are able to follow the movement of this money-capital, as it is used to purchase means of production and labor-power, arriving back at capital in the sphere of production where, as productive capital, the capitalist exploitation of the worker occurs.

From money-capital to productive-capital to commodity-capital and back to money-capital—there is the circuit of capital as a whole that permits the reproduction of capital as the premise of capitalist production. Commodity and money in this respect are produced as commodity-capital and money-capital. Volume 2 ends with Marx's reproduction models, where he explores conditions for the successful realization of the value and surplus value that emerge from the sphere of production.

By understanding this continuing circuit of capital, we recognize that the capital that appears as a premise for capitalist production does not drop from the sky or otherwise from outside the circuit of capital. Even, indeed, if capital were to come *initially* from another source, Marx insisted that "the mere continuity" of this process of production and circulation converts all capital into "capitalized surplus-value." That is, it is the result of the exploitation of workers.[23] This is how the premise of capital is reproduced in capitalism as an organic system: "It is itself presupposed, and proceeds from itself to create the conditions of its maintenance and growth."

Thus, not only does the successful sale of commodities permit the capitalist to satisfy his own consumption desires and to replace the capital invested in the means of production (that is, simple reproduction), but it also creates the conditions for the growth of his capital. In order to drive beyond all barriers to this growth, Marx explained that capital struggles to extend and intensify the workday and to increase productivity relative to wages through development of productive forces. By increasing the rate of exploitation of workers and extracting increased surplus value from them, *expanded* reproduction or accumulation of capital is possible. Thus, the premise of the growth of capital is clear—exploitation of wage-laborers within the sphere of capitalist production and the realization of surplus value in the sphere of circulation.

The Wage-Laborer as Premise

In capitalism as an organic system, capital as premise is the product of the system itself. So also is the other premise of the system, the wage-laborer. In capitalism as an organic system, wage-laborers are not the result of the disintegration of other, pre-capitalist systems. They are not people formed outside of capitalism. Accordingly, "bloody discipline," "police methods," and "state compulsion" are not required in capitalism as an organic system to ensure their submission to capital.[24] On the contrary, with the development of capitalism as an organic system, they have already been subordinated to capital. Rather than abstract wage-laborers, they are already the products of capital.

So what is the nature of the workers produced by capital? While capital develops productive forces to achieve its preconceived goal (the growth of profits and capital), Marx pointed out that "all means for the development of production" under capitalism "distort the worker into a fragment of a man," degrade him, and "alienate him from the intellectual potentialities of the labour process."[25] *Capital* explains the mutilation, the impoverishment, the "crippling of body and mind" of the worker "bound hand and foot for life to a single specialized operation" that occurs in the division of labor characteristic of the capitalist process of manufacturing. But did the development of machinery end that crippling of workers? Marx's response was that under capitalist relations such developments *complete* the "separation of the intellectual faculties of the production process from manual labour."[26] Thinking and doing become separate and hostile, and "every atom of freedom, both in bodily and in intellectual activity," is lost.

A particular type of person is produced in capitalism as an organic system. Producing within capitalist relations is what Marx called a process of a "complete emptying-out," "total alienation," the "sacrifice of the human end-in-itself to an entirely external end."[27] Accordingly, we need money, the true need that capitalism creates; we need money in order to fill the vacuum of our lives with things. We are driven to consume. In addition to producing commodities and capital itself, capitalism thus produces a fragmented, crippled human being, whose enjoyment consists in possessing and consuming things—more and more things. Consumerism is not an accident within capitalism. Capital constantly generates new needs for workers, and it is upon this, Marx noted, that "the contemporary power of capital rests"; in short, every new need for capitalist commodities is a new link in the golden chain that links workers to capital.[28]

This is the other premise of capitalism as a system of reproduction—a particular person always available to be exploited by capital. Is it likely that people crippled by the capitalist process of production can spontaneously grasp the nature of this destructive system? On the contrary, capitalism reproduces the worker's dependence upon capital. As the result of generations of workers having sold their labor-power to the capitalist, "the social productivity of labour" has been transposed "into the material attributes of capital"; the result is that "the advantages of machinery, the use of science, invention, etc. . . . are deemed to be the *attributes of capital*."[29] Accordingly, rather than producing a working class that wants to put an end to capitalism, capital tends to produce the working class it needs, workers who treat capitalism as common sense. As Marx explained in *Capital*:

> The advance of capitalist production develops a working class which by education, tradition and habit looks upon the requirements of that mode of production as self-evident natural laws. The organization of the capitalist process of production, once it is fully developed, breaks down all resistance.[30]

To this Marx added that capital's generation of a reserve army of the unemployed "sets the seal on the domination of the capitalist over the worker." That constant generation of a relative surplus population of workers means, he argued, that wages are "confined within limits satisfactory to capitalist exploitation, and lastly, the social dependence of the worker on the capitalist, which is indispensable, is secured."[31] Accordingly, Marx concluded that the capitalist can rely upon the worker's "dependence on capital, which springs from the conditions of production themselves, and is guaranteed in perpetuity by them."[32]

Things, we conclude, remain recognizably what they are because in capitalism as an organic system every economic relation is reproduced "in its bourgeois economic form." In capitalism as an organic system, capital subordinates "all elements of society to itself." Think about the working class in this picture. Production under capitalist relation creates fragmented, crippled human beings. Capitalism separates thinking and doing for the worker. It produces a working class that looks upon capital's requirements as "self-evident natural laws." It breaks down all resistance to capital. It reproduces the "indispensable" social dependence of the worker on the capitalist. Who could deny that Marx's *Capital* maintains that capitalism as an organic system produces and reproduces its essential premise of wage-labor "in its bourgeois economic form" . . . *in perpetuity*?

In perpetuity? Surely something is missing when we consider capitalism as an organic system. Actually, much is missing in this intellectual construct. One obvious example is that in the concrete whole that is capitalism there is the continuing destruction of pre-capitalist relations of production, the expropriation of peasant producers, the extraction of surpluses from outside the organic system of capitalism—indeed, all of the processes that were critical in "so-called primitive accumulation of capital." They are not part of Marx's conception of capitalism as an organic system.

And that points to the *limited purpose* of this intellectual construct, which is the identification of the essential elements of capitalism as a system of reproduction based upon the capitalist exploitation of the wage-laborer. However, given this limited purpose, we need to ask whether this conception of capitalism as an organic system contains hidden problems, ones that obscure its premises and prevent us from recognizing elements that point beyond capitalism to a new system.

4

Crises and Non-Reproduction

Think about the picture of the reproduction of capitalism in perpetuity. What about the promised inevitable crisis of capitalism? How can we reconcile the idea that capitalism inevitably will be transcended, that is, *non*-reproduced, with *Capital*'s powerful description of the socially dependent working class that capital produces and reproduces in perpetuity?

Perhaps intuitively recognizing this paradox, or perhaps because this is their proclivity, Marxist economists have focused upon the *other* element in the capital-relation, the side of capital. Their chosen task: to demonstrate that the non-reproduction of capitalism occurs because *capital* cannot be reproduced in perpetuity. Because of its internal contradictions that are reflected in its inherent tendency for crisis, capital, and thus the capital-relation, comes to an end.

Crises are always possible in a commodity-money economy. In contrast to a barter economy, sale and purchase are not immediately linked in capitalism because of the existence of money as the intermediary. Following a sale, the money received by the commodity seller, whether it be the capitalist or the worker, need not be immediately turned into purchase of a commodity. Because that seller can "defer the retransformation of money into commodity," therein lies the possibility of the general overproduction and crisis denied by J. B. Say and the political economists who abstract from money. "At a given moment, the supply of all commodities can be greater than the demand for all commodities," Marx pointed out, "since the demand for the general commodity, money, exchange value, is greater than the demand for all particular commodities."[1] In such a case, "the crisis occurs not only because the commodity is unsaleable, but because it is unsaleable within a *particular period of time*."[2] Demonstrating the possibility of capitalist crisis was easy for Marx—and trivial.

Rather than a matter of mere contingency, the question that interested Marx was what makes crises in capitalism *necessary*. What leads capitalists to defer purchase, what interrupts the accumulation of capital (and, indeed, the simple reproduction of capital)? Two different types of crisis theories have been favored explanations of Marxist economists. One focuses upon the interaction of the production and circulation of capital—in particular, the problem of realizing the surplus value latently generated in the sphere of capitalist production, that is, the phenomenon of overproduction. The other emphasizes the difficulty of generating sufficient surplus value in production relative to capital invested, and it stresses an inevitably falling rate of profit as capitalism develops. For both theoretical arguments, inherent tendencies for economic imbalances interfere with the reproduction of capital, one of the premises of the capital-relation, and thus point toward the non-reproduction of capitalism.

Overproduction

Successful completion of a circuit of capital, Marx demonstrated in his reproduction exercises in Volume 2 of *Capital*, requires a particular balance between, on the one side, the value of commodities produced in the two basic sectors—means of production and articles of consumption—and, on the other side, the money intended for purchase of those specific sets of commodities. Such a balance of production and realization of surplus value is possible, Marx argued in the *Grundrisse*, so long as specific proportions and internal relations are respected. At any given point, he proposed, there is an "inner division" of necessary and surplus labor and of direct labor and means of production that mandates that "the exchange of capitals among one another takes place *in specific and restricted proportions*."[3] In short, there are structural requirements for that balance of production and realization of surplus value.

However, capitalism is a commodity-money economy and not a planned system that can ensure the necessary conditions for equilibrium. Individual capitalists act as if there are no structural conditions (no locked room). This immediately introduces the possibility that those specific and restricted proportions will be violated. Exchange of commodities and money "does not change the inner characteristics of realization," but it gives those requirements "a reciprocally independent form, and thereby lets their unity exist merely as an inner necessity, which must therefore come forcibly to the surface in crises."[4] Thus, it is the violation of those inner requirements inherent in the "obscure" structure of the system that produces crisis: "There would be no crisis without this inner unity of factors that are apparently indifferent to each other."[5] Although in exchange the elements appear indifferent and independent of each other, "their inner necessity becomes *manifest* in the crisis, which puts a forcible end to their seeming indifference towards each other."[6]

What makes such a crisis predictable? Specific to capitalism is that the conditions for the realization of surplus value differ significantly from the conditions for the production of surplus value. While every capitalist would like "the workers of other capitalists to be the greatest consumers possible of his own commodity," Marx explained that each tries to restrict the consumption of his own worker, "his ability to exchange, his wage, as much as possible." And, the latter side, the side of the production of surplus value, is the essence of the capital-relation: "The relation of *every* capitalist to *his own* workers is the *relation as such* of *capital and labour*, the essential relation."[7] Since capital must sell commodities in order to realize surplus value, what occurs in the sphere of production comes back to haunt capital in the sphere of circulation. "Contradiction in the capitalist mode of production," Marx noted in Volume 2 of *Capital*. "The workers are important for the market as buyers of commodities. But as sellers of their commodity—labour-power—capitalist society has the tendency to restrict them to their minimum price."[8]

Accordingly, since the capitalist sphere of circulation is not an abstract, externally juxtaposed sphere of circulation but, rather, one determined by capitalist relations of production, its "antagonistic conditions of distribution" produce a "constant tension between the restricted dimensions of consumption on the capitalist basis, and a production that is constantly striving to overcome these immanent barriers."[9] When capital comes up against those barriers in the sphere of circulation, capitalist production comes to a halt; this is because capital "posits necessary labour only *to the extent and in so far as* it is surplus labour and the latter is *realizable* as *surplus value*."[10] Thus, the combination of capital's drive to expand production as if there are no limits and the limits to the market given by the restriction upon workers generates "*overproduction*, the fundamental contradiction of developed capital."[11]

Nevertheless, limits upon workers' consumption are not the proximate (as opposed to ultimate) cause of crises of overproduction because such limits are always present. So what changes to produce crises? Overproduction crises develop because of the victories of capital in the sphere of production, that is, its success in increasing the rate of exploitation and thereby altering the "inner division" of necessary and surplus labor. The ability of capital "to reduce the relation of this necessary labour to surplus labour to the minimum," Marx pointed out, posits "a new barrier to the sphere of exchange."[12] Overproduction arises precisely because the consumption of workers "does not grow correspondingly with the productivity of labour."[13] All other things equal, this change in the "inner division" of necessary and surplus labor generates a tendency for overproduction to emerge in the sector producing articles of consumption (Department II) and to spread from there.

All other things, however, are not necessarily equal immediately. If capitalist expenditures upon means of production rise sufficiently, the "specific and restricted proportions" necessary for balance will not be violated. Expanded production in Department I, in short, can support the realization of surplus value. Marx made this very point in his reproduction models in Volume 2 of *Capital*: "The capitalist class as a whole . . . must itself cast into circulation the money needed to realize its surplus value." Not only was this point not paradoxical, "it is in fact a necessary condition of the entire mechanism."[14] Rather than crisis, the immediate effect of an increase in the rate of exploitation may be expansion and boom.

Ultimately, the apparent independence of the means of production and the conditions for realizing surplus value proves to be illusory. Continued investment in Department I must be validated by the limitless growth of demand for articles of consumption. Although the demand for new means of production may appear "adequate and sufficient," Marx indicated that "its inadequacy shows itself as soon as the final product encounters its limit in direct and final consumption."[15] As that occurs, the effects are multiplied in Department I: "The *overproduction* of coal is implied in the *overproduction* of iron, yarn etc. (even if coal was produced only in proportion to the production of iron and yarn etc)."[16] Under these conditions, "capital already invested is in fact massively unemployed, since the reproduction process is stagnant." Then comes "the inevitable crash."[17]

Thus, the initial boom is entirely consistent with the limits upon workers' consumption inherent in capitalism. As Marx indicated in his Volume 2 comment on the contradiction of the capitalist mode of production, "Further contradiction: the periods in which capitalist production exerts all its forces regularly show themselves to be periods of over-production; because the limit to the application of the productive powers is not simply the production of value, but also its realization."[18] The consistent pattern, he insisted in *Capital*, was one of "feverish production, a consequent glut on the market, then a contraction of the market, which causes production to be crippled."[19]

Crises thus put "a forcible end" to the apparent separation of the production and realization of surplus value. While they reveal the existence of particular barriers inherent in the nature of capitalism, "transitory over-abundance of capital, over-production and crises" in themselves do not bring capitalism to an end.[20] Rather, Marx viewed crises as "momentary, violent solutions for the existing contradictions, violent eruptions that re-establish the disturbed balance for the time being."[21] *And that is the point—overproduction crises are a regular part of the process of reproduction.* "Permanent crises," Marx indicated, "do not exist."[22] Rather, the emerging crisis acts "to restore the correct relation between necessary and surplus labour, on which, in the last analysis, everything rests."[23]

The Falling Rate of Profit

In contrast to crises of overproduction that revolve around the question of the realization of produced surplus value, emphasis upon the falling rate of profit stresses the tendency of the value of capital expended upon means of production to rise more rapidly than surplus value extracted from workers—thus, inadequate production of surplus value. Further, in contrast to a focus upon periodic crises of overproduction, those who concentrate upon the falling rate of profit (FROP) tend to stress a permanent crisis of capitalism.

It is well known that Marx was not the first to identify a tendency for the rate of profit to fall "with the progress of capitalist production." Indeed, he described this as "the most important law of political economy."[24] In the case of Adam Smith, this tendency was the result of the growth in the quantity of capital, that is, the increase in the supply of capital. For Ricardo, on the other hand, diminishing returns in agriculture over time increased the level of necessary labor and thereby reduced the rate of surplus value (which he identified as the rate of profit). Here, for classical political economy, was the spectre haunting capitalism: "What disturbs Ricardo," Marx commented, "is the way that the rate of profit, which is the stimulus of capitalist production and both the condition for and driving force in accumulation, is endangered by the development of production itself."[25] Indeed, "the whole of the Ricardian and Malthusian school is a cry of woe over the day of judgement this process would inevitably bring about."[26] Could one wonder at "the terror which the law of the declining rate of profits inspires in the economists"?[27]

However, what does it mean to speak about an "important law of political economy"? For a student of Hegel "law" has a specific meaning—it is what we postulate as we search for regularities in the chaos and noise of appearance. Thus, Hegel asserted: "Appearance and law have one and the same content."[28] Empiricism is its source, and what is missing from law as such is an understanding of *inner* connections and necessity. Lenin grasped this in his reading of the *Science of Logic*: "Law is the enduring (the persisting) in appearances." The concept of law is one of the stages of cognition, but every law is "narrow, incomplete, approximate."[29] And this was explicitly the point Marx made in one of his earliest works. Political economy, he proposed, has its laws but "it does not *comprehend* these laws"; we have to go beyond external appearances "to grasp the intrinsic connection."[30]

FROP was one such law, a law that the economists formulated but did not understand. Contrary to their explanations, Marx explained that the real source of the pattern observed by political economy was that central to the development of capitalism is the substitution of means of production for direct living labor, that is, the growth in the technical composition of capital. As capitalism develops, past labor (dead labor) plays an increasingly important role in production relative to present, living labor. But since the source of surplus value, Marx argued, is the exploitation of living workers, the rise in the technical composition of capital brings with it a relative reduction in that portion of capital that yields surplus value.

Thus, the change in the value-composition of capital (the rise in the organic composition of capital) was Marx's inner explanation for the law that classical political economy had identified. Through his critique of political economy, Marx revealed what was hidden from the political economists and explicitly rejected their explanations for their law. However, Marx proceeded then to stress that there were other tendencies in capitalism as it developed that counteracted and weakened the tendency for the rate of profit to fall. In particular, two such tendencies were (1) increases in the rate of surplus value; and

(2) economies in constant capital, with the former increasing surplus value relative to capital expended and the latter, lowering constant capital relative to surplus value. These, however, were not independent and external factors disturbing the trajectory of the system. *Rather, they were negative feedbacks inherent in the system.*

Consider the logic behind Marx's inner explanation for the tendency for the rate of profit to fall. With the substitution of a machine for a given number of workers, past labor rises relative to present labor both in the form of fixed capital and also with the increased quantities of semi-manufactured inputs and "raw and ancillary materials to be transformed into products in the same time by the same number of workers, i.e. with less labour."[31] Assuming the average value of means of production and the average value of labor-power constant, the organic composition of capital will mirror this increase in the technical composition of capital while the rate of surplus value is constant. Under these conditions, the capital required in the sphere of production rises relative to the surplus value produced, and the rate of profit must fall.

Yet the rise in the technical composition of capital is intrinsically linked to increased productivity, an obvious point when we think about the increased inputs that a given number of workers are able to transform into finished products. So, consider the effect of this increased productivity. Marx insisted in Volume 1 of *Capital* that increases in productivity (both directly and indirectly) in the sector producing articles of consumption have the effect of driving down necessary labor and raising the rate of surplus value. This, after all, is the central point of Marx's theoretical exposition of the concept of relative surplus value.

In short, the rise in the technical composition of capital generates a particular feedback from increased productivity—a tendency for the rate of surplus value to increase.[32] It would appear at first sight, accordingly, that this "counter-tendency" would counteract the tendency of the rate of profit to fall; that is, the combination of an increase in the organic composition of capital and an increased rate of surplus value would have an indeterminate effect on the rate of profit. However, if the rise in the organic composition of capital mirrors the rise in the technical composition of capital, no increase in the rate of surplus value (even if it were to continue to the point where almost all new value is captured by capital in the form of surplus value) can counteract that increase in the organic composition of capital. Here, though, is the begged question. For the movement of the organic composition of capital to mirror that of the technical composition of capital, the average value of means of production must be unchanged. But why should the average value of means of production remain unchanged if increases in the technical composition of capital increase productivity?

Better than most of his disciples, Marx understood that the argument for an ultimately declining rate of profit involves ignoring the feedback of productivity increases upon the value of constant capital. Writing in the *Grundrisse*, where the basic elements of his FROP argument were first developed, Marx argued that the composition of capital would *remain the same* if "productivity increases at the same time not only in the given branch of production, but also in its conditions." On the other hand, a rise in the constant component of capital emerges "if the objective conditions of production . . . remain unchanged in value."[33] Marx's argument for the growth in the composition of capital explicitly rested upon the uneven development of productivity:

> If the force of production increased simultaneously in the production of the different conditions of production, raw material, means of production and means of subsistence, and in the [branches of production] determined [by them], then their growth would bring about no change in the relation between the different component parts of the capital.[34]

He returned to this same point several years later in his *Economic Manuscripts of 1861–63*. There, he extended calculations for the rate of profit and demonstrated that, depending upon assumptions about relative productivity changes, (a) the rate of profit falls, (b) is constant or (c) rises.[35] Of all the cases he considered there, the only one that corresponds to the FROP story introduced in chapter 13 of Volume 3 of *Capital* is where productivity in the sector producing material inputs is explicitly assumed constant. Accordingly, Marx concluded from these exercises that it would appear "that the rate of profit cannot *fall* unless" (a) the value of labor-power rises (Ricardo's assertion); or (b) "there is a rise in the *value of constant capital in relation to variable*. And the latter would appear to be restricted to cases where the productive power of labour does not rise *equally* and *simultaneously* in all the branches of production which contribute to produce the commodity."[36] Finally, you can see the same point twice in Marx's exposition of FROP in *Capital* 3, where he admitted that the rate of profit might remain the same (a) if "the productivity of labour cheapens all the elements of constant and variable capital to the same extent"; and (b) "if the increase in productivity affected all the ingredients of the commodity uniformly and simultaneously."[37]

Equal productivity changes in all sectors? No falling rate of profit. Indeed, Marx explicitly added that "the rate of profit could even rise, if the rise in the rate of surplus value was coupled with a significant reduction in the value of the elements of constant capital, and fixed capital in particular."[38] Once we consider capitalism as a system, FROP appears as a tendency whose realization depends upon the relative strength of feedback loops associated with productivity changes, feedback that is internal to the system rather than an external counterforce. In this respect, Marx proposed with respect to FROP that "the law operates therefore simply as a tendency, whose effect is decisive only under particular circumstances and over long periods."[39]

What are those "particular circumstances" and why only over long periods? Significantly, Marx proposed that it was only in "isolated cases" that cheapening of "all the elements of constant and variable capital to the same extent" prevents the rise in the organic composition of capital and the fall in the rate of profit. Rather than affecting "all ingredients of the commodity uniformly and simultaneously," Marx stressed that in practice "the development of labour productivity is far from uniform in the various branches of industry and, besides being uneven in degree, often takes place in opposite directions."[40]

Is there a systemic reason, though, for productivity increases to lag in the sector producing means of production? Not when it comes to fixed capital (for example, machinery), and Marx offered none. But consider the other side of constant capital. Raw material, Marx pointed out, "forms a major component of constant capital," and with growing productivity, its value "forms an ever-growing component of the value of the commodity produced." For instance, if productivity in wool spinning is tripled, "then, provided the conditions of production of the wool remained the same ... three times as much capital would have to be expended in wool production." Obviously, without "a corresponding decline in raw material's value arising from the increasing productivity of the labour applied in its own creation," the result will be a significant growth in constant capital.[41]

But would that corresponding growth in productivity be forthcoming? Considering the growth in the technical composition of capital, Marx asked if ten times as much cotton can be worked on by a spinner as the result of technical change, why should not the cotton itself *also* be produced ten times as productively, "that is, why should the *value* ratio not remain the same?" His answer was unequivocal:

> To this it is quite easy to answer that some kinds of raw materials, such as wool, silk, leather, are produced by animal organic processes, while cotton, linen, etc are produced by vegetable organic processes and capitalist production has not yet succeeded, and never will succeed in mastering these processes in the same way as it has mastered purely mechanical or inorganic chemical processes. . . . As far as coal and metal (wood) are concerned, they will become much cheaper with the advance of production; this will however become more difficult as mines are exhausted, etc.[42]

Very simply, Marx repeatedly noted that it was "easy to comprehend" lagging (and even declining) productivity in agriculture and the extractive industries because in these cases "the productivity of labour is also bound up with natural conditions, which are often less favourable as productivity rises—as far as that depends on social conditions." Precisely because "we not only have the social productivity of labour to consider but also its natural productivity which depends on the natural conditions within which labour is carried on," the feedback of productivity from increases in the technical composition of capital in such cases (and thus also its effect as counter-tendency) is weakened.[43]

Was Marx, then, fleeing "from economics to seek refuge in organic chemistry," as he described Ricardo's falling rate of profit theory?[44] Hardly. Whereas Ricardo's argument was based upon diminishing productivity and a fall in the rate of surplus value, for Marx the tendency of the rate of profit to fall was associated with rising productivity and a rising rate of surplus value. Further, whereas Ricardo "thinks that agriculture must become unproductive absolutely," for Marx the fall in the rate of profit would occur not, for example, because "the yield of cotton cultivation had declined, but only that it had not become more productive in *the same ratio* as cotton manufacturing. Therefore only a *relative* reduction in its productivity, despite the absolute increase in it."

Such a relative decline due to "the natural conditions within which labour is carried on," Marx proposed, only demonstrates "that industry and agriculture do not develop to the *same degree* in *bourgeois* production. If they do not do this, that alone is sufficient to explain the decline in the rate of profit."[45] Is this, then, sufficient to explain the ultimate and inevitable non-reproduction of capitalism? Perhaps. "Over long periods," this relative lag in productivity may mean that the falling rate of profit will have a "decisive" effect.

Well before this lonely last hour, however, Marx stressed that natural conditions affect the course of capitalist development. "Plant and animal products, whose growth and production are subject to certain organic laws involving naturally determined periods of time, cannot suddenly be increased in the same degree as, say, machines and other fixed capital, coal, ore, etc." Thus, it is "indeed unavoidable when capitalist production is fully developed, that the production and increase in the portion of constant capital that consists of fixed capital, machinery, etc. may run significantly ahead of the portion consisting of organic raw materials, so that the demand for those raw materials grows more rapidly than their supply and their price therefore rises."[46]

In boom periods, accordingly, relative underproduction of raw materials is predictable: "Although the raw material would have been sufficient for the *old level of production*, it will be insufficient for the *new*. . . . It is a case of *overproduction of fixed capital*."[47] Capital, which develops "a capacity for sudden extension by leaps and bounds," comes up against barriers, not only in the sphere of circulation but also in a barrier "presented by the availability of raw materials."[48] And this brings with it a fall in the rate of profit: all other things equal, "the rate of profit falls or rises in the opposite direction to the price of the raw material."[49]

But barriers are not limits. They can be transcended, and capital responds in two ways to a crisis that is the result of the raw material barrier. First, the crisis itself lowers the organic composition of capital because of the destruction and devaluation of capital due to stagnation and crisis brought about by the falling rate of profit. "Under all circumstances," Marx commented, "the balance will be restored by capital's lying idle or even by its destruction, to a greater or lesser extent."[50] Second, capital is itself not passive when faced by the barrier of the relative underproduction of raw materials. Thus Marx noted that among the effects of rising raw material prices are that (1) these raw materials are supplied from a greater distance; (2) their production is expanded; (3) substitutes are now employed that were previously unused; and (4) there is more economical use of waste products.[51] Precisely because relative underproduction of raw materials produces rising prices and relatively rising profit rates in those sectors, capital inevitably flows to those sectors. Capital, in short, responds to this barrier by seeking ways to posit its growth again:

> Hence exploration of all of nature in order to discover new, useful qualities in things . . . new (artificial) preparation of natural

objects, by which they are given new use values. The exploration of the earth in all directions, to discover new things of use as well as new useful qualities of the old; such as new qualities of them as raw materials etc; the development of the natural sciences, hence, to their highest point . . . is likewise a condition of production founded on capital.[52]

To the extent capital succeeds in driving beyond the underproduction of raw materials, it enters a phase characterized by relatively declining raw material values, a lower value-composition of capital and a rising rate of profit. In short, cycles. or long waves. What FROPists tend to forget is that capital responds to barriers to its growth by finding ways to go beyond all barriers. Precisely because capital is an actor, it has a tendency to restore the disturbed balances. And that is the essential point to be grasped: *capital has a tendency to be self-correcting, self-regulating.* Capitalism will not self-destruct as the result of its economic contradictions (however clever the mathematical proof).

Economic Crises and Homeostasis

"In the face of constantly displacing influences," Levins and Lewontin asked, "how do things remain recognizably what they are?" Their response was posed in terms of negative and positive feedback loops. A positive feedback occurs if an initial event sets processes in motion that magnify the original change; in contrast, negative feedback exists when the opposite occurs, when the effect is to diminish that initial impact. In considering the above crisis theories, I have pointed out the (often ignored) negative feedbacks that generate the tendency for "homeostasis, the self-regulation observed in physiology, ecology, climatology, the economy and indeed all systems that show any persistence."

The "dialectical task," Levins and Lewontin argued, is to explain how "things are the way they are because of the temporary balance of opposing forces."[53] What is the relation, then, between these two crisis arguments and the homeostasis of capitalism? If these crises were strong enough or if circumstances were such as to generate positive feedback, they could indeed intensify the initial effects and pose the question of the non-reproduction of capitalism. However, in the organic system of capitalism, Marx concluded that the capitalist can rely upon the worker's "dependence on capital, which springs from the conditions of production themselves, and is guaranteed in perpetuity by them."[54] This is the negative feedback that ensures the reproduction of capitalism as an organic system.

Rather than pointing to the nonreproduction of capitalism, capital's tendency for crises that are self-correcting and the workers' tendency to look upon capital as necessary may combine to *strengthen* the reproduction of capitalism; they are opposing forces that act to produce the homeostasis of the system. Whatever its source, every crisis successfully navigated increases the acceptance of capital's requirements as common sense and reinforces what Lukács called the "immaturity of the proletariat." As Lukács commented:

> This gives rise to the delusion that the "laws" of economics can lead the way out of a crisis just as they lead into it. Whereas what happened in reality was that—because of the passivity of the proletariat—the capitalist class was in a position to break the deadlock and start the machine going again.[55]

The Crisis of the Earth System

Let us consider, though, the real crisis that we face—the crisis of the Earth System. You don't need to be a Marxist to recognize that humanity and all forms of life at this time face a crisis of existence. But it helps. It helps because Marxist theory has always understood that capitalism by its very nature contains within it the spectre of this crisis and that there is no solution as long as capital prevails.

The work of John Bellamy Foster (and other writers especially associated with *Monthly Review*) has highlighted what was always present (but relatively ignored for so long) in Marx's analysis of capitalism, namely, capital's inherent tendency to destroy the earth and its inhabitants. Whereas Marx hoped for a possible world in which successive generations might inherit the earth "in an improved state," we have now approached the point where the idea of successive generations itself is in question.[56]

In "The Capitalist Nightmare and the Socialist Dream," I described nature as one of capital's "waste products."[57] Whereas nature has its own metabolic process through which it converts various inputs and transforms them into the basis for its reproduction, the particular metabolic process that occurs within capitalist production is one in which human labor and nature are converted into surplus value for capital's reproduction. Labor and nature are mere means for capital, and the result is that capitalist production undermines "the original sources of all wealth—the soil and the worker."[58] Indeed, the very nature of production under capitalist relations violates "the metabolic interaction between man and the earth"; it produces "an irreparable rift in the interdependent process of social metabolism, a metabolism prescribed by the natural laws of life itself."[59]

This irreparable rift, however, does not produce a crisis of capital. The crisis of the Earth System does not in itself produce falling profit rates. The deformed outputs of capital cost it nothing. Rather, a crisis of human beings and nature affects capital as such only if society attempts to shift some of the burden of the metabolic rift it creates to capital. Unchecked, capital's relation to the natural world is precisely the same as its relation to workers: "*Après moi le deluge!* is the watchword of every capitalist and every capitalist nation. Capital therefore takes no account of the health and the length of life of the worker, unless society forces it to do so."[60]

But can the society that capital produces, a society in which the working class looks upon the requirements of capital as "self-evident natural laws," prevent the deluge? There are no self-correcting tendencies with respect to the crisis of the Earth System. Rather than the negative feedback generated by economic crises, the crisis of the Earth System generates positive feedback. Things get worse. And the result is that "the original system can no longer persist as it was. The system may go into wider and wider fluctuations and break down."[61]

As we have seen, the working class produced in capitalism as an organic system tends to ensure the reproduction of capitalism in perpetuity. In doing so, that working class ensures the non-reproduction of humanity and the Earth System. To the extent that workers are the products of capital, neither homeostasis nor an escape from the crisis of the Earth System are options.

PART III

THE SECOND PRODUCT

5

Never Forget the Second Product

Something significant is missing in *Capital*. Or, rather, *someone*. As noted in my Introduction, "The worker is not present as the subject who acts for herself against capital." Present is the worker produced by capital, the crippled worker who is the premise and result of capitalist production, the worker who looks upon capital's requirements as common sense … in perpetuity. Left out of the theory presented in *Capital*, with the exception of that brief glimpse of the importance of workers acting in common in chapter 10, is what was always central to Marx's revolutionary dynamics, namely "revolutionary practice," the simultaneous change in circumstances and self-change.

Hegel and Revolutionary Practice

Marx developed his concept of revolutionary practice in the course of his comprehension and critique of Hegel. Hegel's declaration that "the truth is the whole" is well known; however, its continuation is less so: "The whole, however, is merely the essential nature reaching its completeness through the process of its own development."[1] Self-development, self-movement, self-activity, this was Hegel's understanding of how the Idea (Spirit, Freedom) advances to its completion through a process of acting upon itself.

Thus, as well as his focus upon an interconnected whole, at the core of Hegel's philosophical system was his emphasis upon a dialectical process through which the Idea drives forward (ultimately to God) by negation of each momentary form of its existence. "The Concept forges ahead," Hegel stressed, by means of the "negative which it carries within itself." This, indeed, was the particular focus of his *Phenomenology*: "We have here modes of consciousness each of which in realizing itself abolishes itself, has its own negation as its result—and thus passes into a higher mode."[2]

Through its activity, the Idea transforms itself and advances. Nowhere is this clearer than in *Phenomenology*'s account of the advance of self-consciousness through the activity of the slave (bondsman) in producing something for his master: "In fashioning the thing, self-existence comes to be felt explicitly as his own proper being." Precisely through his labor, "the bondsman becomes aware, through this rediscovery of himself by himself, of having and being a 'mind of his own.'" The advance to freedom of self-consciousness for Hegel, we see, occurs through "the formative activity of work," through labor.[3]

The idealism and mysticism of Hegel so apparent here was challenged by Feuerbach's materialist reversal of subject and predicate, his insistence that, rather than ideas and concepts, human beings were the true subjects. In contrast to the philosophy of Hegel—and characteristic of what Lenin called "Hegel materialistically turned upside-down"—Feuerbach declared: "Man *is* self-consciousness."[4] And soon, following in Feuerbach's stream, Marx applied that inversion of Hegel's subject and predicate in his *Contribution to the Critique of Hegel's Philosophy of Law*: "Hegel everywhere makes the idea the subject and turns the proper, the actual subject, such as 'political conviction' into a predicate." Indeed, Marx pointed out, "the correct method is stood on its head."[5]

So what happens if Hegel's account of the self-development and self-movement of the Idea is "materialistically turned upside-down"? While declaring that "Feuerbach is the only one who has a *serious, critical* attitude to the Hegelian dialectic and who has made genuine discoveries in this field," Marx nevertheless saw genius in Hegel's *Phenomenology*.[6] "The outstanding achievement of Hegel's *Phenomenology* and of its final outcome, the dialectic of negativity as the moving and generating principle," Marx proposed, "is thus first that Hegel conceives the self-creation of man as a process." He "grasps the essence of *labour* and comprehends objective man—true, because real man—as the outcome of man's *own labour*." Hegel "grasps labour as the *essence* of man ... [as] *man's coming-to-be for himself* within *alienation*, or as *alienated* man." Since Hegel turns everything on its head, though, "the only labour which Hegel knows and recognizes is *abstractly mental* labour." Thus, "Hegel conceives labour as man's act of self-genesis," but only "within the sphere of abstraction."[7]

While the mere reversal of subject and predicate could yield the vision of abstract Man advancing to perfection through his activity, Marx was aided in going beyond this simple negation by the empirical orientation of his fellow Feuerbachian, Frederick Engels. Political agitator and author of reports on developing communist movements and then of *The Condition of the Working Class in England*, where, among other things, he introduced the concept of the reserve army of the unemployed and described strikes as "the military school of the working-men in which they prepare themselves for the great struggle," Engels began his collaboration with Marx in 1844 by working with him on *The Holy Family*, a critique of the idealism of German philosophers (but which also contained glimpses of the real struggles of workers).[8]

In their joint work that followed, *The German Ideology*, the two revolutionaries continued their critique of German speculative philosophy for which ideas and concepts rule. In it they also proceeded further to an explicit critique of Feuerbach's substitution of abstract "Man" for Hegel's "Idea." Rather than combating disembodied ideas with *better* disembodied ideas, Marx and Engels focused upon real living human beings formed on the basis of historically developed productive forces and social relations. Rather than the independence of ideas, they insisted that the producers of ideas and conceptions were "real, active men, as they are conditioned by a definite development of their productive forces and of the intercourse corresponding to these, up to its highest forms." [9] Thus, in place of an idealistic conception of history, on the one hand, and a "contemplative materialism" without history, on the other, Marx and Engels introduced a materialist conception of history.

Given the central purpose of this work, *The German Ideology* focused upon the definite conditions (productive forces and social relations) that produce the ideas of definite human beings. But it was never an argument that those real, active human beings were mere bearers of particular productive forces and the social relations to which they corresponded. On the contrary, Marx and Engels stressed the importance of a revolution by the working class against the existing conditions of the time. This revolution was necessary "not only because the *ruling* class cannot be overthrown in any other way, but also because the class *overthrowing* it can only in a revolution succeed in ridding itself of all the muck of ages and become fitted to found society anew."[10] Through its revolutionary activity, in short, the working class transforms itself.

Can we conceive of revolution *without* a change in the working class itself? In *The German Ideology*, Marx and Engels stressed an extended process in which the working class develops itself and unites through its struggles: "The proletarians arrive at this unity only through a long process of development in which the appeal to their right also plays a part. Incidentally, this appeal to their right is only a means of making them take shape as 'they,' as a revolutionary, united mass."[11] Thus they rejected the argument of Max Stirner, one of the German ideologists, who separated revolution on the one hand, and change in the working class on the other. For Stirner, it was possible that "the communist proletarians who revolutionize society and put the relations of production and the forms of intercourse on a new basis . . . remain 'as of old.'" The idea that workers remain unchanged, however, was contrary to their concept of the revolutionary process: "In revolutionary activity," Marx and Engels responded to Stirner, "the changing of oneself coincides with the changing of circumstances."[12]

This last phrase from *The German Ideology* recalls a central point in Marx's preparatory notes, his *Theses on Feuerbach*. These notes provide useful insight into *The German Ideology* as well as Marx's subsequent work. In contrast to his earlier celebration of Feuerbach, here Marx explicitly parted company with Feuerbach for failing to consider the practical activity of real human beings. Feuerbach's materialism, Marx proposed, was a *contemplative* materialism, one whose concept of "the essence of man" was that of an individual abstracted from society. But from what perspective was Marx's critique? In the very first of his theses, Marx made his point clearly: "in contradistinction to materialism, the *active* side was set forth abstractly by idealism—which, of course, does not know real, sensuous activity as such."[13] Very simply, Marx's critique of Feuerbach embraced Hegel's "outstanding achievement" in his *Phenomenology*—the grasp of "the self-creation of man as a process," the understanding that "real man" is "the outcome of man's *own labour*." Hegel's insight, in short, was the thread that Marx would pursue: "labour as man's act of self-genesis," but no longer "within the sphere of abstraction."[14]

Thus, in contrast to Feuerbach's understanding of the "essence of man" as an abstract individual, Marx in his theses focused upon the activity of real individuals who were the ensemble of the social relations within a particular society. To escape idealism and various forms of mysticism, Marx insisted that it was necessary to understand the "inner strife and intrinsic contradictoriness" of this society. The existing society must be "both understood and revolutionized in practice," that is, "destroyed in theory and in practice."[15] And, as Marx had learned from Hegel—"materialistically turned upside-down," of course—through their activity, those real human beings transform themselves.

Obviously, if the self-creation of real human beings is a product of their own activity, then people are not changed by changing circumstances *for* them. Despite the "materialist doctrine" that human beings are the product of circumstances and that therefore changed human beings are the product of changed circumstances, if changed circumstances are presented as gifts from above, it leaves people "as of old." That doctrine of change from above, Marx declared in the

Theses, divides "society into two parts, one part of which is superior to society." Characteristic of Marx's revolutionary materialism, in contrast, was the key link of human development and practice: "The coincidence of the changing of circumstances and of human activity or self-change can be conceived and rationally understood only as *revolutionary practice*."

Understanding the Second Product

Human activity, self-change—the two cannot be separated. To refer to one is to imply the other.[16] From the concept of revolutionary practice we learn that there are always two products of human activity—the change in circumstances and the change in the human being. Every act of production, every human activity, thus has as its result joint products, both the change in the object of labor and the change in the laborer himself. As Marx noted in the *Grundrisse*, in the very act of producing, "The producers change, too, in that they bring out new qualities in themselves, develop themselves in production, transform themselves, develop new powers and new ideas, new modes of intercourse, new needs and new language."[17] Similarly, the recognition of the worker as outcome of his own labor is present in *Capital*'s discussion of the labor process—there the worker "acts upon external nature and changes it, and in this way he simultaneously changes his own nature."[18]

In short, there is always a *second* product of human activity. Not only the material product of activity but also the human product. But that human product is not an abstract human being because human activity always occurs under particular social relations, and this necessarily affects the particular nature of the second product. Consider, for example, the nature of the second product resulting from activity under capitalist relations of production. Where "it is not the worker who employs the conditions of his work, but rather the reverse, the conditions of work employ the worker," a particular second product emerges. Head and hand become separate and hostile in this capitalist inversion, "this distortion, which is peculiar to and characteristic of capitalist production" in which "every atom of freedom, both in bodily and in intellectual activity" is lost. Through the destruction of existing (and potential) capacities, capital produces the workers it needs. It produces workers who are fragmented, degraded, and alienated from "the intellectual potentialities of the labour process." Those crippled and deformed human beings are the second product of capital.[19]

Under a different set of productive relations, however, Marx envisioned a quite different second product. In contrast to the society in which the worker exists to satisfy the need of capital for its growth, Marx in *Capital* explicitly evoked "the inverse situation, in which objective wealth is there to satisfy the worker's own need for development."[20] In contrast to the worker under capitalist relations who "actually treats the social character of his work, its combination with the work of others for a common goal, as a power that is alien to him," here associated producers expend "their many different forms of labour-power in full self-awareness as one single social labour force." In this "inverse situation," rather than the crippling of workers, here workers *develop* their capacities: "When the worker co-operates in a planned way with others, he strips off the fetters of his individuality, and develops the capabilities of his species."[21]

Thus, if workers democratically decide upon a plan, work together to achieve its realization, solve problems that emerge and shift in this process from activity to activity, they engage in a constant succession of acts that expand their capacities. For workers in this inverse situation, there is the "absolute working-out of his creative potentialities," the "complete working-out of the human content," the "development of all human powers as such the end in itself."[22] Collective activity under these relations produces "free individuality, based on the universal development of individuals and on their subordination of their communal, social productivity as their social wealth."[23] As Marx concluded in the *Critique of the Gotha Programme*, with the development of this new relation of associated producers, the productive forces of people have "increased with the all-round development of the individual, and all the springs of co-operative wealth flow more abundantly."[24] Workers here satisfy their "own need for development."

Class Struggle as Production

All other things equal, the people produced within particular relations of production tend to be premises for the reproduction of those relations. As we saw, the second products of capital are people who look upon the requirements of capital as "self-evident natural laws," common sense. However, work under capital is not the only relation in which those workers produce themselves. The key link of human development and practice points to another product within capitalism: through their struggles, workers change themselves and make themselves fit to create a new world. Thus, Marx's message to workers in 1850 was that "you will have to go through 15, 20, 50 years of civil wars and national struggles not only to bring about a change in society but also to change yourselves, and prepare yourselves for the exercise of political power."[25] Over two decades later (after the defeat of the Paris Commune), he continued to stress the inseparability of human activity and self-change: the working class knows that "they will have to pass through long struggles, through a series of historic processes, transforming circumstances and men."[26]

Struggle, in short, is a process of production—one in which workers produce themselves differently. Although capitalist relations of production determine the working class as a class-in-itself, Marx in *The Poverty of Philosophy* explained that through its struggles, "this mass becomes united, and constitutes itself as a class for itself."[27] By informing themselves about their own interests and acting in common, workers can emerge (as *The German Ideology* predicted) "as a revolutionary, united mass."[28] And this is something only they can do. Precisely because revolutionary practice is the way that workers transform themselves, Marx criticized sects (which possess all the answers in their pockets to the suffering of the masses): "Here [referring to Germany], where the worker is regulated bureaucratically from childhood onwards, where he believes in authority, in those set over him, the main thing is *to teach him to walk by himself.*"[29]

No one has described the intrinsic link between their activity and their self-change better than Engels. Even though they had lost the battle over the Ten Hours Bill, he argued that workers changed significantly in the course of that struggle:

> The working classes, in this agitation, found a mighty means to get acquainted with each other, to come to a knowledge of their social position and interests, to organise themselves and to know their strength. The working man, who has passed through such an agitation, is no longer the same as he was before; and the whole working class, after passing through it, is a hundred times stronger, more enlightened, and better organised than it was at the outset.[30]

And, as noted in my Introduction, this is what Marx demonstrated in Chapter 10 of *Capital*: developing from "passive, though inflexible and unceasing" resistance, workers proceeded to engage in open class struggle. Through continuous pressure by organized workers, it was possible to achieve legislative limits upon the workday. Legislative victories, though, don't bring the struggle over the workday to a close. Even where the "latent power of the working classes of the United States" had produced legislation for an eight-hour workday, in 1868 Marx pointed out that "the resistance of rebellious capital" meant that workers in New York were "engaged in a fierce struggle" to *enforce* that law. Indeed, as the struggle in New York demonstrated, "even under the most favourable political conditions all serious success of the proletariat depends upon an organisation that unites and concentrates its forces."[31]

The second product of this struggle is that workers are no longer the same as they were before. They are "stronger, more enlightened, and better organised." They *learn* in the process of struggle. The struggle over the workday, Marx noted in chapter 10, proved "conclusively that the isolated worker, the worker as 'free' seller of his labour-power, succumbs without resistance once capitalist production has reached a certain stage of maturity." Accordingly, workers learn that they must struggle against separation and isolation; they must transform their relations and themselves if they are to make any gains in the protracted "civil war between the capitalist class and the working class."[32]

The Ensemble of Acts and Capacities

Through their struggles against capital, workers develop their capacities. They make themselves fit to undertake new struggles. In this dialectical relation of acts and capacities, acts create capacities, capacities enable acts. The first of these sides was stated succinctly by Lucien Sève: "Every developed personality appears to us straight away as *an enormous accumulation of the most varied acts through time*."[33] In turn, he defined capacities as "the ensemble of actual potentialities, innate or acquired, to carry out any act whatever and whatever its level."[34]

It would be an error, however, to identify this dialectic of acts and capacities by only considering the activity of workers as wage-laborers. As I argued in *Beyond* Capital (in chapter 8, "The One-Sidedness of Wage-Labour"), "To examine the human being *only* insofar as he is wage-labourer is clearly one-sided." It reproduces the error of the political economy that Marx early criticized, that of treating the proletarian "only as a *worker*" and not considering "him when he is not working, as a human being."[35] As the "ensemble of social relations," workers are the product of *all* their relations and of their activity and struggles within them. Sève, after all, refers to an "*accumulation of the most varied acts*" in the development of capacity and to that capacity as the potential to carry out *any act whatever* and whatever its level.

So what builds that capacity? We cannot ignore the effect of relations such as patriarchy, racism, ethnicity, sexual orientation, and citizenship status in forming our existing capacities nor the effect of struggles within those spheres in altering capacities.[36] Rather than privileging one side, we have to take into account all sides of workers and all their struggles to satisfy their need for development. If workers organize to fight for higher wages or against racism or within their community to struggle against gentrification, they develop new capacities. The worker is "no longer the same as he was before." There is an important political lesson here: social movements are multiple sites for developing the capacities of the working class, and we forget that at our peril.

Consider where the thread of Marx's concept of revolutionary practice has led us. With the focus upon acts and capacities, we put flesh upon that insight that Marx found in Hegel's *Phenomenology*: "the self-creation of man as a process." Capacity, we understand, is a stock that is expanded (or contracted) as a result of particular acts, and that stock is the basis for a flow of acts. Of course, the existence of a large capacity, that is, a high potential for carrying out acts, doesn't mean that all of that capacity will be necessarily utilized. There is always the potential of *unutilized* capacity. And if particular capacities are unutilized, they tend to atrophy, even if they have been built up in the past.[37] For capacity not to wither away, it must be continuously renewed by acts.[38] Revolutionary practice requires permanent revolution.

The expanded reproduction of capacity can be utilized in many different ways.[39] Those who struggle against sexism, for example, can strengthen themselves to struggle against capital because they have changed themselves, and those who do not struggle remain "as of old." Simultaneous changing of circumstances and self-change, that concept of revolutionary practice, is absolutely central to understanding Marx. What, though, are the theoretical implications of its disappearance from *Capital*? Our task is to understand first how that disappearance occurred, and second, its effects upon Marxist theory.

6

The Burden of Classical Political Economy

As we have seen, class struggle determines the length of the normal workday and that in the process of struggle workers transform themselves. Are the other critical elements in the determination of the degree of exploitation—the real wage and productivity—similarly determined by class struggle? On the contrary, the real wage is assumed to be "given" in *Capital*: there are no wage struggles; there is no civil war between the capitalist class and the working class to determine the level of real wages.

In the absence of wage struggles, what is the nature of the working class that capital produces? Such struggles, Marx argued in 1853, are the "indispensable means of holding up the spirit of the labouring classes, of combining them into one great association against the encroachments of the ruling class, and of preventing them from becoming apathetic, thoughtless, more or less well-fed instruments of production." In their absence, he predicted, the working class "would be a heart-broken, a weakminded, a worn-out, unresisting mass."[1] And he made the same point in 1865: workers who do not struggle over wages are "degraded to one level mass of broken wretches past salvation." They thereby "disqualify themselves for the initiating of any larger movement."[2] What Engels called "the military school of the working-men in which they prepare themselves for the great struggle" is obviously not present.

Insofar as the workers introduced in *Capital* do not transform themselves through wage struggles, these "more or less well-fed instruments of production" are the products of capital, the workers that capital needs, workers who guarantee the reproduction of capital "in perpetuity." But what happened in *Capital* to the working class that struggled over the workday and developed its capacity and organization in the process? Very simply, the voice of the worker that we hear in chapter 10 of *Capital* was again "stifled," this time by what Marx took from classical political economy.

Hats and Men

Consider the value of the commodity that the worker sells to the capitalist. What the worker sells, Marx argued in *Capital*, is his labor-power (rather than labor), and (following in the footsteps of classical political economy), its value is "determined, as in the case of every other commodity, by the labour-time necessary for the production, and consequently also the reproduction, of this specific article."[3] Accordingly, "as in the case of every other commodity," the value of this commodity will fall with reductions in the labor-time necessary for its production, that is, with increases in productivity.

There is, in short, symmetry in the treatment of labor-power and other commodities, a symmetry in which Marx followed Ricardo, whom he credited as the first to formulate accurately relations (laws) that Marx elaborated in *Capital*.[4] Ricardo expressed this symmetry in his *Principles of Political Economy* as follows:

Diminish the cost of production of hats, and their price will ultimately fall to their new natural price, although the demand should be doubled, tripled or quadrupled. Diminish the cost of subsistence of men, by diminishing the natural price of the food and clothing by which life is sustained, and wages will ultimately fall, notwithstanding that the demand for labourers may very greatly increase.[5]

"The cynical Ricardo," Marx called him in 1844. But he was not commenting upon a personal characteristic of Ricardo; rather, Ricardo's teaching was the perspective of "*English political economy*, i.e. the scientific reflection of English economic conditions."[6] That political economy, Marx commented, viewed "man as *worker*, as a *commodity*" and was indifferent to the production of man as "a *mentally* and physically *dehumanised* being." Indeed, its only interest in workers was with respect to their direct relation to capital.[7] But the cynicism of political economy, Marx explained in his *Poverty of Philosophy*, was just a statement of "the facts" in capitalism. Quoting the above passage from Ricardo, Marx commented:

Doubtless, Ricardo's language is as cynical as can be. To put the cost of manufacture of hats and the cost of maintenance of men on the same plane is to turn men into hats. But do not make an outcry at the cynicism of it. The cynicism is in the facts and not in the words which express the facts.[8]

But what was that "cost of subsistence of men" that determined the value of labor-power? It "can be resolved," Marx indicated, "into the value of a definite quantity of the means of subsistence," and we can assume that set of use-values to be constant: "The quantity of the means of subsistence required is given at any particular epoch in any particular society, and can therefore be treated as a constant magnitude."[9] What *precisely* was that definite quantity of means of subsistence? Irrelevant, Marx explained: "Whether one assumes the level of workers' needs to be higher or lower is completely irrelevant to the end result. The only thing of importance is that it should be viewed as given, determinate."[10]

The Ricardian Default

This assumption of a given and determinate standard of necessity underlies the "Ricardian Default." For Ricardo, this assumption provided the direct link between productivity and profit and was the source of the central tendency he identified—the falling rate of profit. Falling productivity (the result of diminishing returns in agriculture), given the constant standard of necessity, meant that more hours of labor were necessary to produce the wage and thus an increase in necessary labor, reduced surplus labor and thus the falling rate of profit—or, more precisely, a falling rate of surplus value.

In the case of Marx, the Ricardian Default underlies his explanation of relative surplus value in *Capital*. Specifically, in this case, if we assume a given set of necessities, productivity increases for those use-values mean that less labor is required to produce the worker and thus, the value of labor-power "varies with the value of the means of subsistence."[11] Further, as Marx explained in chapter 16, since "the value of labour-power and surplus value vary in opposite directions," an increase or decrease in the productivity of labor means that "surplus value moves in the same direction" as productivity.[12]

Marx's acceptance of the Ricardian Default, however, does more than determine his explanation of the development of relative surplus value. It also led to his description of the central tendency of capital. "Capital," he declared, "therefore has an immanent drive, and a constant tendency, towards increasing the productivity of labour in order to cheapen commodities and, by cheapening commodities, to cheapen the worker himself." [13]

As we can see, characteristic of the Ricardian Default is that any link between productivity and the standard of life of workers is precluded by assumption. As the result of the assumption of a given standard of necessity, in the one case workers cannot lose as the result of decreases in productivity and, in the other case, workers cannot gain as the result of increases in productivity. In both cases, it is by assumption, and only by assumption, that capital alone benefits or loses as productivity changes.

That assumption underlying the Ricardian Default, Marx proposed, can be traced back to the Physiocrats. Precisely because they had made the "strict necessaire," the "minimum of wages," "the equivalent of the necessary means of subsistence," the pivotal point in their theory, Marx declared them to be "the true fathers of modern political economy." By treating the minimum of wages as fixed and as a given magnitude, "the Physiocrats transferred the inquiry into the origin of surplus value from the sphere of circulation into the sphere of direct production, and thereby laid the foundation for the analysis of capitalist production." And, this assumption of a fixed set of necessities, of that given subsistence wage, he commented, was followed by Adam Smith "like all economists worth speaking of."[14]

"The Facts" and the Assumption

By the time Marx wrote *Capital*, he had come to understand that there was a difference between this classical premise of a fixed set of necessities and "the facts." Certainly, he accepted the classical premise for his presentation of the concept of relative surplus value in chapter 12 of Volume 1. However, *outside of this theoretical chapter*, Marx elsewhere commented in *Capital* that workers are able to expand their consumption of means of subsistence under the appropriate conditions. The fixed character of workers' needs, he indicated in Volume 3, "is mere illusion. If means of subsistence were cheaper or money-wages higher, the workers would buy more of them."[15] Similarly, in Volume 2, he explained that with rising real wages "the demand of the workers for necessary means of subsistence will grow. Their demand for luxury articles will increase to a smaller degree, or else a demand will arise for articles that previously did not enter the area of their consumption."[16] Further, he pointed out in Volume 1 that, with higher wages, workers "can extend the circle of their enjoyments, make additions to their consumption fund of clothes, furniture, etc., and lay by a small reserve fund of money."[17]

We need, accordingly, to distinguish between the theoretical exposition of relative surplus value and passing observations made in the course of his historical illustration of capital's "immanent drive." Not only was Marx clear that there is not a fixed set of necessities in practice, but he also observed in chapter 16 of Volume 1 that rising productivity did *not* necessarily lead to the development of relative surplus value.[18] This was not a new revelation: this important caveat, in fact, had been developed at length in his *1861–63 Economic Manuscripts*. There, Marx revealed that his theoretical presentation in *Capital* with respect to the effect of productivity increases was only one of *three* possible cases. In the first case, the worker "receives same quantity of use values as before. In this case there is a fall in the value of his labour capacity or his wage. For there has been a fall in the value of this quantity, which has remained constant." In the second case, "There is a rise in the amount, the quantity, of the means of subsistence . . . but not in the same proportion as in the worker's productivity." Accordingly, the real wage rises but its value falls. That is, there is both rising real wages and relative surplus value.

"Finally the third CASE," where productivity and the standard of necessity rise at the same rate:

> The worker continues to receive the same value—or the objectification of the same part of the working day—as before. In this case, because the productivity of labour has risen, the quantity of use-values he receives, his real wage, has risen, but its value has remained constant, since it continues to represent the same quantity of realised labour time as before. In this case, however, the surplus value too remains unchanged, there is no change in the ratio between the wage and the surplus value, hence the proportion [of surplus value] to the wage remains unchanged.[19]

In this third case, Marx explained, "there would be no CHANGE in surplus value, although the latter would represent, just as wages would, a greater quantity of use values than before." Three possibilities! Yet, only the *first* case where workers were limited to a fixed set of use-values entered into Marx's explanation of the concept of relative surplus value. Marx's assumption of the given standard of necessity in *Capital* was contrary to "the facts" he knew so well, that workers within capitalism can obtain more means of subsistence and thus can be the beneficiaries of productivity increases.

So, now we need to explain the mystery. Why did Marx accept the classical assumption in *Capital* that the worker "receives same quantity of use values as before"? Unlike so many of his disciples, Marx understood this was an explicit assumption, one that must be *removed*. As he explained to Engels at the very point he formulated his projected six-book plan for his *Economics*, "Wages are invariably assumed to be at their minimum."[20] Similarly, he was explicit in the *Grundrisse*: "For the time being, necessary labour supposed as such; that the worker always obtains only the minimum of wages." [21] This, he indicated in his letter to Engels, was a temporary assumption: "the rise or fall of that minimum will be considered under wage labour." Further, in the *Grundrisse* he explained that the standard of necessary labor, while treated as fixed, may change and that "to consider those changes themselves belongs altogether to the chapter treating of wage labour."

Was Marx's intent to explore such matters subsequently in a separate study of wage-labor part of an obsolete or superseded plan? In his subsequent *Economic Manuscript of 1861–63*, for example, Marx indicated that the question of "movements in the level of the workers' needs" was not to be explored here "but in the doctrine of the wages of labour." For now, he insisted that it was essential that the level of workers' needs be viewed as "given, determinate. All questions relating to it as not a given but a variable magnitude belong to the investigation of wage labour in particular."[22] Further in that manuscript, Marx noted that his investigation proceeded from the assumption that wages are "only reduced by the DEPRECIATION of that labour capacity, or what is the same thing, by the cheapening of the means of subsistence entering into the workers' consumption" and that any other reason for a reduction in wages was "not part of our task" and "belongs to the theory of wages."[23]

A few years later, Marx repeated the same point. In "The Results of the Immediate Process of Production," he explained: "The level of the necessaries of life whose total value constitutes the value of labour-power can itself rise or fall. The analysis of these variations, however, belongs not here but in the theory of wages."[24] Nor was this his last reference to the book on wage labor. In Chapter 20 of Volume 1 of *Capital*, Marx noted that "the special study of wage-labour, and not, therefore, to this work" is where an exposition of the forms of the wage belongs.[25] In short, over and over again, Marx insisted that it was necessary to remove that assumption and to do so in his separate study of wage-labor.

But why *wait*? Why did he postpone the removal of this assumption? His answer was based upon methodological considerations: first the "general capital-relation" had to be developed. Since variations in the standard of necessity "do not touch its general relationship to capital," to understand the nature of capital and the capital-relation, "the only thing of importance" was to treat the standard of necessity "as given, determinate." Variations in the standard of necessity, he insisted, do not "alter anything in the general relationship."[26] Accordingly, as he had indicated in the *Grundrisse*, in his letter to Engels and in his comments on the Physiocrats, all that was needed for the study of capital was to assume that "the worker always obtains only the minimum of wages." It followed that changes in the standard of necessity are not part of the study of capital and "belong to the investigation of wage labour in particular."

"Only by this procedure," Marx explained to Engels, "is it possible to discuss one relation without discussing all the rest." He elaborated this approach in the *Grundrisse*: "All of these fixed suppositions themselves become fluid in the further course of development. But only by holding them fast at the beginning is their development possible without confounding everything." What appears fixed and static, in short, is revealed in a dialectical presentation to be fluid and changing. Only "for the time being" was it assumed that "the worker always obtains only the minimum of wages"; and this fixed supposition was only held "fast at the beginning."

Unfortunately, while seeming plausible methodologically, Marx's justification for maintaining his assumption loses credibility given that he had already assumed the standard of necessity given in the *Poverty of Philosophy*, the *Communist Manifesto*, and *Wage-Labour and Capital*—all before reacquainting himself with Hegel's *Science of Logic* (the source of his methodological renewal). To postpone relaxation of the classical assumption to a later "special study of wage-labour" meant that *Capital* remained at the level of classical political economy with its symmetry of hats and men.

Whereas *Beyond* Capital stressed the "missing book on wage-labour," I am now convinced that I was mistaken in thinking that it was the failure of subsequent Marxists to recognize the importance of that missing book that produced a one-sided Marxism. The problem was deeper. Marx himself was *wrong* to think that retaining the assumptions of classical political economy did not "alter anything in the general relationship." By accepting the Ricardian Default and the symmetry of hats and men for his theoretical exposition of relative surplus value, Marx reverted to a "pre-Marxian" perspective and distorted the "general capital-relation."

Money and Wage-Labor

Think about the critique of political economy with which *Capital* begins. At its core is the question of money. For classical political economists, money didn't matter. It was a mere veil for the real, concrete economy. This was why they could embrace the quantity theory of money (with money determining only nominal price levels), why they effectively treated a commodity-money economy as a barter economy (thereby precluding the possibility of crises), and why they were able to move directly from coefficients of production (how many men to make a hat, how many hats to make a man) to profits without passing money.

In contrast, Marx solved what he called "the riddle of money." He demonstrated that, rather than being juxtaposed externally to commodities, money was inherent in the concept of the commodity. Developed logically from the commodity and unleashing more of its qualities, money did not supersede the commodity but existed alongside and interacted with it. Money, Marx revealed, was essential for the "metamorphosis of commodities," the movement from one commodity in the hands of its owner via the medium of money to a second commodity that could be a use-value for the owner of the first. Without stressing the distinct existence and centrality of money, like the classical political economists we do not understand the inherent possibility of crisis or the nature of capital as a social relation.

But there is more. The place of money in Marx's analysis points to the error in treating the production of hats and men symmetrically. Money doesn't matter for the production of hats, a vertically integrated process of production extending from primary products, which contingently may be interrupted by the equivalent exchange of intermediary inputs, to the completed use-value. But we cannot talk about the production and reproduction of the wage-laborer without incorporating the place of money.

Rather than existing solely within a sphere of production, the production of labor-power involves a complex sequence encompassing (a) the moment of production of articles of consumption; (b) the payment of money-wages to the worker; (c) a moment of circulation in which the worker exchanges his or her money for articles of consumption; (d) a second moment of production in which those use-values (as well as concrete, uncounted labor) are consumed in order to prepare labor-power for exchange; and (e) the sale of labor-power to the capitalist.[27] By treating the two processes symmetrically, *only* the first of these moments in the production of labor-power is considered. In classical political economy, the cost of production of the consumption bundle leapfrogs over several moments to become the cost of production of the worker (leaving the latter a mere footnote to the former).

In contrast, as we have seen, Marx understood the importance of money with respect to workers. The suggestion of a fixed standard of necessity, he insisted, is "mere illusion. If means of subsistence were cheaper or money-wages higher, the workers would buy more of them."[28] Again, the higher money-wages are relative to money-prices, the more that workers "can extend the circle of their enjoyments, make additions to their consumption fund of clothes, furniture, etc., and lay by a small reserve fund of money" and the more the worker is able to participate in "higher, even cultural satisfactions . . . widening the sphere of his pleasures" and gaining "his only share of civilization which distinguishes him from the slave."[29] For Marx, unlike the classical economists, money obviously mattered.

But it did not when it came to the theoretical exposition of relative surplus value in *Capital*. By following classical political economy in precluding gains for workers from productivity increases, the crucial difference between a wage-laborer and a slave was obscured. The slave, Marx explained in the "Results of the Immediate Process of Production," receives the means of subsistence he requires, "which are fixed both in kind and quantity—i.e. he receives use-value." But that is not true for the wage-laborer. In contrast to the slave, the wage-laborer receives means of subsistence in the shape of money, and "it is the worker himself who converts the money into whatever use-values he desires; it is he who buys commodities as he wishes and, as the owner of money, as the buyer of goods, he stands in precisely the same relationship to the sellers of goods as any other buyer."[30] Rather than the product of a fixed set of use-values, the wage-laborer here appears as a subject with money and with his own goals. Rather than turning men into hats, the theoretical discussion of relative surplus value in *Capital* turns the relation of wage-laborer into that of a slave.

Of course, the slave does not benefit from increased productivity. Only his owner does. And, given Marx's acceptance of the Ricardian Default, in *Capital* only the capitalist does. The conceptual symmetry of hats and men leads us far astray. Yes, increased productivity at any stage in the production of hats will disrupt the equivalence of embodied social labor and money and will lead to a fall in value of hats: "Diminish the cost of production of hats, and their price will ultimately fall to their new natural price." Similarly, increased productivity in the production of means of subsistence in general leads to a reduction in their value. However. rather than the fall in "the cost of subsistence of men" leading to a fall in wages, "workers would buy more" means of subsistence. With money-values falling, all other things equal, real wages rise!

Here, however, is the problem. If wage-laborers (unlike slaves) are the immediate beneficiaries of productivity increases, *how is relative surplus value possible*? Capital cannot rely upon the assumptions of classical political economy and never has. What is to be done?

7

Capital's Need to Separate Workers

Marx's acceptance of the Ricardian Default explains why the worker disappeared as a subject after chapter 10. In place of workers who develop their strength by struggling in common, we have the "apathetic, thoughtless, more or less well-fed instruments of production" about which Marx despaired. But we need to think about this disappearance not simply as a deficiency but as a sign that there is something important outside Marx's logical construct of capitalism as an organic system.

If there is indeed something outside that organic system from which we gained our understanding of capital and its logic, then that system is itself merely a part of the whole, and our understanding of it and its elements is potentially faulty. As I explained in chapter 2, our intellectual construct in that case may misrepresent the real concrete:

> Recognizing that only the whole is the truth, Levins and Lewontin insist that "we always have to be aware that there is more out there that might overwhelm our theories and thwart our best intentions." What is excluded from our mental construct, indeed, may infect our concept of the whole and its parts.

In particular, failing to incorporate new sides of categories under investigation and "seizing upon one side of a dichotomous pair or a contradiction as if it were the whole thing" can infect our concept of the whole with "one-sidedness."

Relative and Absolute Surplus Value

In chapter 12 of *Capital*, relative surplus value is revealed through a simple arithmetical exercise. Given the length of the workday (determined by class struggle) and the standard of necessity (fixed by assumption), a rise in productivity reduces the hours of necessary labor and thus increases the relative portion of surplus labor. The social relations underlying the emergence of relative surplus value are not immediately apparent, no more than they were for Ricardo. But the same cannot be said with respect to absolute surplus value.

We have seen that Marx followed "all economists worth speaking of," that is, classical political economy, with respect to the standard of necessity. However, he did not do so when it came to determination of the workday. There was nothing to follow: classical political economy did not recognize the workday as a variable. Accordingly, Marx was free to forge his own important path, a path that immediately revealed the coercion at the core of capitalist relations of production.

In developing the concept of absolute surplus value, Marx introduced the essential characteristic of capitalist production—the coercive relationship of "supremacy and subordination" of capital over wage-laborers.[1] We cannot think about capitalist relations without understanding the centrality of this supremacy and subordination. Does that coercive relation disappear when we leave absolute surplus value to consider relative surplus value? Does the worker's rebellion against that coercion really disappear?

Why doesn't the "antinomy of right against right" essential to the determination of the normal workday apply as well to the determination of the standard of necessity? It *would* if the working-class subject revealed in chapter 10 had not been yanked off the stage. And it *should* apply if Marx's critique of political economy is to reflect the now open, now hidden "struggle between collective capital and collective labour, i.e. the class of capitalists, and collective labour, i.e. the working class."[2]

Without classical political economy's stifling assumption, we would recognize that capital faces a working class that develops its capacity and organization through its struggles, a working class that is transforming social relations among its members. And that raises the question as to whether the absence of that particular part infects our theoretical conception of the whole.

Reproducing Supremacy and Subordination

We know that it is inherent in capital to attempt to grow. But the accumulation of capital generates particular types of feedback. In "the historical genesis of capitalist production," accumulation of capital drove up money-wages. As a result, "the consumption-fund of the workers" expanded, and this negative feedback checked the ability of capital to grow. Under these conditions, for capital to obtain the funds for further accumulation, it had to defeat the working class. How did it do that when "the subordination of labour to capital was only formal, i.e. the mode of production itself had as yet no specifically capitalist character"? By using the state to reduce and keep money-wages down. Through "state compulsion" and "police methods" limiting wages and banning the combination of workers, capital was able to confine "the struggle between capital and labour within limits convenient for capital."[3]

Feedback from the accumulation of capital takes different forms with the development of a mode of production with a "specifically capitalist character." Here, rather than rising money-wages expanding "the consumption-fund of the workers," increases in productivity brought about by manufacture and then machinery and the factory system cheapen the means of subsistence. There is here the possibility that the reduced value of commodities would expand that consumption fund as workers struggle to secure the benefits of rising productivity through increased real wages. There is here the possibility, in short, of negative feedback that prevents the emergence of relative surplus value.

Yet characteristic of the specifically capitalist mode of production is that it generates positive feedback that tends to separate workers and to check a rise in real wages. Within the workplace, this mode of production destroys the capacities of workers and increases the antagonism of head and hand; within society, it expands the reserve army of labor both by incorporating workers with a lower historic standard of necessity and by displacing workers through the substitution of machinery for direct labor. Increased separation of workers by the "constant generation of a relative surplus population keeps the law of the supply and demand of labour, and therefore wages, within narrow limits which correspond to capital's valorization requirements." Accordingly, Marx concluded that, rather than requiring state compulsion, in this case "the movement of the law of supply and demand of labour on this basis completes the despotism of capital."

The coercive relation of supremacy and subordination thus is preserved through the market within the organic system of capitalism. The market does this by reconciling the actions of individuals with the logic of capital. Through individual actors, the inner laws of capital are made real.[4] For example, when an individual capitalist lowers his cost of production relative to competitors by increasing productivity, Marx noted, "he contributes towards increasing the general rate of surplus value" even though this is no part of his intention.[5] His action, too, "forces his competitors to adopt the new method." Thus, "the seemingly independent influences of the individuals, and their chaotic collisions," is how the inner laws of capital appear "as external necessity" imposed by the market.[6]

Through their individual attempts to grow, Marx argued that "the many capitals force the inherent determinants of capital upon one another and upon themselves." In short, the market, that is, competition, "executes the inner laws of capital; makes them into compulsory laws toward the individual capital, but it does not invent them. It realizes them." Competition is what is apparent on the surface. But what is the inner law that is realized? If we are to understand "the way in which the immanent laws of capitalist production manifest themselves in the external movement of the individual capitals [and] assert themselves as themselves as the coercive laws of competition," we need to "grasp the inner nature of capital."[7]

Yet it is not only the actions of individual capitalists that execute the "general and necessary tendencies" of capital. The same is true of the actions of individual workers. As the General Council of the First International declared, "What the lot of the labouring population would be if everything were left to isolated, individual bargaining, may be easily foreseen. The iron rule of supply and demand, if left unchecked, would speedily reduce the producers of all wealth to a starvation level."[8]

The reasoning was quite clear: competition between workers "allows the capitalist to force down the price of labour"; it brings with it an increase in the length and intensity of the workday of employed workers, forcing them "to submit to overwork."[9] In contrast to the side of capital, the efforts of wage-laborers as individuals to act in their self-interest run counter to the interests of wage-labor as a whole. In piece-work, for example:

> The wider scope that piece-wages give to individuality tends to develop both that individuality, and with it the worker's sense of liberty, independence and self-control, and also the competition of workers with each other. The piece-wage therefore has a tendency, while raising the wages of individuals above the average, to lower this average itself.[10]

Further, the self-interest of the individual wage-laborer engaged in piece-work similarly leads to the intensification of labor: "Given the system of piece-wages, it is naturally in the personal interest of the worker that he should strain his labour-power as intensely as possible; this in turn enables the capitalist to raise the normal degree of intensity of labour more easily."[11] Thus, acting in their individual interest and competing among themselves, workers do not express the inner tendencies of wage-labor but, rather, the inner tendencies of capital.

Insofar as workers are atomized and compete, they act in the interest of capital. Accordingly, Marx concluded that "the competition among workers is only another form of the competition among capitals."[12]

The Blind Rule of the Supply-and-Demand Laws

Neither individual capitalists nor individual workers grasp the "general and necessary tendencies of capital." Instead they see the "forms of appearance" of the inner laws, and they are conscious that they are driven by the market and must obey it if they are to survive.[13] These everyday notions, the common consciousness of the agents of production themselves, are the starting point for the political economists of capital. Those economists, Marx argued, do "nothing more than to translate the peculiar notions of the competition-enslaved capitalist into an ostensibly more theoretical and generalized language, and attempt to demonstrate the validity of these notions."[14] For the political economy of capital, markets rule. "The blind rule of the supply and demand laws," Marx declared, forms "the political economy of the middle class."[15]

That blindness means that the political economy of capital cannot grasp central characteristics of capitalism. With its stress upon markets—the "realm of Freedom, Equality, Property and Bentham"—it does not see the supremacy and subordination inherent in capitalist production since it views capitalist and worker as contractors who freely exchange equivalents.[16] Further, since individual capitals compete with each other by lowering *all* their costs (raw materials, labor, interest, rent, etc.), nothing privileges the exploitation of workers. Accordingly, the political economy of capital necessarily is also blind with respect to the centrality of the exploitation of workers.

Precisely because the political economy of capital is based upon the everyday consciousness of capitalists, it also does not understand the inevitability of crises. Atomistic capitals do not proceed from consciousness of "the interconnection of the reproduction process"; they think only of their own actions and not of the structural requirements for the reproduction of the system. Accordingly, without a grasp of the inner requirements of the system as a whole—for example, the characteristics of the "locked room"—the political economists of capital are blind to the underlying general and necessary tendencies of capital.

Insofar as the political economy of capital expresses the perspective of capital, it aids in the reproduction of capitalism as an organic system. It supports the reproduction of that "working class which by education, tradition and habit looks upon the requirements of that mode of production as self-evident natural laws."[17] Left to "the blind rule of the supply and demand laws," the despotism of capital over workers is completed, now and forever.

Divide, Divide

Recall, however, the workers of chapter 10 who subsequently disappeared. As soon as workers learn the secret of the market and competition and begin to act in common against its effects, "the more does their very function as a means for the valorization of capital become precarious."[18] We see here the unstated condition of the reproduction of the organic system of capital, namely, the *atomization of the working class*. That (and only that) is what permits "the blind rule of the supply and demand laws" to ensure the reproduction of capitalism.

Accordingly, once the working class begins to transform itself from a class in itself into a class for itself through its struggles, "the blind rule of the supply and demand laws which form the political economy of the middle class" is revealed as capital's class view. Opposing that political economy is "social production controlled by social foresight, which forms the political economy of the working class."[19] In contrast to the political economy of capital that is based upon atomistic individuals, implicit in the political economy of the working class is conscious activity based upon a conception of the whole, that is, where associated producers expend "their many different forms of labour-power in full self-awareness as one single social labour force."[20]

Workers must combine for that political economy of the working class to be made real. Through their struggles over the workday, workers clearly learned this critical lesson, the necessity to organize and to negate competition among themselves. Organized workers, Marx understood, do not permit wages "to be reduced to the absolute minimum; on the contrary, they achieve a certain quantitative participation in the general growth of wealth."[21] That, Engels commented, was the great merit of the trade unions: "They tend to keep up and to raise the standard of life."[22]

Just as important as achieving this result is the transformation of workers in the course of struggling. "Everyday struggles" are essential in preventing workers, Marx stressed, from being "downgraded to one level of broken wretches past salvation." They make possible "the initiating of any larger movement." There are limits to such "guerrilla fights." Marx concluded, in *Value, Price and Profit*, that "Trade Unions work well as centres of resistance," but they need to use "their organized forces as a lever for the final emancipation of the working class."

That, after all, was the goal. As the First International declared in its "Provisional Rules," the aim was "the economical emancipation of the working classes." Achievement of that goal "had hitherto failed from the want of solidarity between the manifold divisions of labour in each country, and from the absence of a fraternal bond of union between the working classes of different countries." Thus, while workers were learning the necessity for combining to fight against the "never-ceasing encroachments of capital or changes in the market," they needed further to learn the unequivocal need for solidarity of the class as a whole.[23]

But capital was also learning a lesson from the struggles of workers; it learned the need to consciously separate and atomize the working class. As soon as workers organize trade unions, as soon as "they try to organize planned cooperation between the employed and the unemployed . . . so soon does capital and its sycophant, political economy, cry out at the infringement of the 'eternal' and so to speak 'sacred' law of supply and demand."[24] Challenged by workers is the view that the requirements of capital are "self-evident natural laws," that is, common sense. Accordingly, capital draws upon its political economists for ideological support. However, capital has never limited itself to the ideological level nor relied solely upon the blind rule of supply and demand.

The ruling classes are "unwilling to be without the weapons of the old arsenal in case some emergency should arise." Capital, we know, does not hesitate to use the state to "take away from the workers the right of association." The 1791 decree in France preventing every combination of workers, for example, was a clear effort to use "state compulsion to confine the struggle between capital and labour within limits convenient for capital." And so too a subsequent act of legislation in France intended to ensure that workers "not be permitted to inform themselves about their own interests nor to act in common" and thereby lessen their dependence upon capital.[25] To "act in common" is precisely what workers must not be permitted to do.

In the "struggle between collective capital and collective labour, i.e. the class of capitalists, and collective labour, i.e. the working class," capital actively searches for ways to prevent workers from acting in common. How better than to foster differences (real and imagined) such as race, ethnicity, nation, and gender and to convert difference into antagonism! Marx certainly understood how capital thrives upon divisions within the working class. That, he declared, is the "secret" of capital's rule. Describing the antagonism between English and Irish workers at the time, Marx explained this is "the *secret of the impotence of the English working class*, despite its organization. It is the secret by which the capitalist class maintains its power. And that class is fully aware of it."[26]

Divide, divide the working class! Capital knows that "the workers' power of resistance declines with their dispersal."[27] However, the need to divide workers is not part of the logic of capital that Marx presented in *Capital*. When Marx says that capital has "an immanent drive, and a constant tendency, towards increasing the productivity of labour in order to cheapen commodities and, by cheapening commodities, to cheapen the worker himself," where is there any consideration of capital's "immanent drive, and a constant tendency" to divide the working class? It remains a secret, albeit one that the capitalist class "is fully aware of." And, as long as that is a secret, it means you do not understand the enemy.

If you do not understand the centrality of capital's need to separate workers, you will not grasp that such characteristics as racism, patriarchy, and xenophobia do not drop from the sky, and you will suggest that we obscure relations of class exploitation by emphasizing these. On the contrary, these characteristics are produced and reproduced within a capitalism that must divide the working class if it is to be reproduced. Silence about "the secret by which the capitalist class maintains its power" disarms the working class and, indeed, betrays it. Rejecting the tendency of some Marxists to treat race and gender oppression as outside the logic of capital, David Roediger correctly argues that "Marx left the production of difference untheorized in a way that we cannot afford to."[28]

Was the theoretical silence about capital's absolute necessity to divide workers a matter of incompleteness rather than a serious flaw of *Capital*? Recall the point from Levins and Lewontin: "Seizing upon one side of a dichotomous pair or a contradiction as if it were the whole thing," can infect our concept of the whole with "one-sidedness."[29] When an element is excluded from our concept of the whole, they predicted, it "may take its revenge in leading us astray."[30] This is precisely what occurred.

The Non-Neutrality of Productive Forces

If capital does not need to divide workers because the standard of necessity is given, this leaves *Capital* with only one explanation of relative surplus value—productivity increases. Once capital's need to divide and separate workers is recognized *explicitly as part of its logic*, however, you understand that the productive forces that capital introduces are not arbitrary or ad hoc; rather, they are particular to capitalist relations of production, to the necessity to reproduce the supremacy and subordination of capital over workers. Marx understood that within the capitalist system, "all means for the development of production undergo a dialectical inversion so that they become means of domination and exploitation of the producers." He certainly did not view as neutral productive forces that degrade the worker "to the level of an appendage of a machine."

If your premise is that all that matters is the growth of productive forces, relations of production disappear from consideration. This is a deformation of Marxism, one that easily fosters the view that the advance of productive forces combined with juridical ownership of the means of production is the basis for the advance of socialism and that we need not concern ourselves with the kinds of people produced under particular relations of production. Indeed, as I proposed in *The Contradictions of "Real Socialism,"* the theoretical inference as to the neutrality of productive forces provides ideological support for a society divided into conductors and the conducted.[31] That theoretical inference is one of the most grievous effects of Marx's discussion of relative surplus value.

Once we understand that inherent in capitalist production is capital's "immanent drive, and a constant tendency" to divide workers, several propositions follow:

- If there is a way to divide the working class, capital will find it and use it. Changes in the organization of production and in the technical composition of capital introduced by capital must be seen in this light.
- When capital initiates such changes in the organization of production, it does so on the premise that it will be the beneficiary, either because of the existing atomism of the working class or the expectation that the change will have that effect.
- If the benefits of productivity increases are to be captured by an organized working class, capital has no interest in developing productive forces. The expanded reproduction of capital has as its premise the separation of the working class.

The separation of the working class is also the premise of the operation of the blind laws of supply and demand. Marx's statement that "the movement of the law of supply and demand of labour" as the result of the replacement of workers by machinery "completes the despotism of capital" has as its premise the atomism of the working class. Given workers who are isolated, atomistic competitors, the "sacred" law of supply and demand ensures that workers are produced in their bourgeois economic form, that is, as the products of capital.[32]

Every combination of the working class, however, "disturbs the 'pure' action of this law."[33] Indeed, it disturbs the "pure" organic system of capitalism and points beyond that mental construct to "social production controlled by social foresight, which forms the political economy of the working class." It points to that society (indeed, that organic system) in which associated producers expend "their many different forms of labour-power in full self-awareness as one single social labor force."

PART IV

CONTESTED

REPRODUCTION

8

Beyond Atomism

The Tragedy of Atomism

Given that the immanent drive and constant tendency of capital is to atomize the working class, what are the effects of this tendency? For the atomized worker, all other workers are competitors; all other workers are enemies insofar as they are competing for the same jobs. All other workers potentially stand between them and the satisfaction of their needs.

Atomized workers may see a logic in joining together with others in the same situation against a "greater enemy," perhaps against workers of other races and ethnicities. Further, in seeking "their immediate, everyday interests," they may even identify their interests with those of their capitalist employers. As Engels pointed out, atomization "restricts the workers to seeing their interest in that of their employers, thus making every single section of workers into an auxiliary army for the class employing them." For example, "The factory worker lets himself be used by the factory owner in the agitation for protective tariffs." The basis for viewing workers from different countries as the enemy is obvious.[1]

Underlying all the behavior of wage-laborers within capitalism is that they do not have an alternative means by which to maintain themselves except by selling their labor-power. Accordingly, for the atomized worker, the "worker's dilemma" within capitalism becomes "do I take a job for lower wages and longer and more intense working conditions or does someone else get it?" Preventing the cooperation of workers is their "division and dispersal," which, Engels commented, "renders it impossible for them to realise that their interests are common, to reach understanding, to constitute themselves into *one* class."[2]

Left to "isolated, individual bargaining," the atomistic wage-laborer thus acts like the *homo economicus* of neoclassical theory, calculating pleasure and pain (as transmitted by price) and considering only that which is rational for him or her as an individual. This is one way in which the real atomism of wage-laborers (which capital strives to produce and reproduce) is reflected in neoclassical theory. Also present is the real counterpart of the logical fallacy of composition: each individual worker attempts to advance his or her individual interest, as if what is true for that worker is all that matters; the result, as the General Council of the First International declared, is that workers as a whole lose.

This is the tragedy of atomism, which is familiar to some in the garb of the so-called tragedy of the commons. As is well known, the latter is intended as a cautionary tale to explain why common property theoretically leads to disaster. Thinking that if I don't take advantage someone else will, each individual peasant chooses to graze an additional animal on the common fields, and the result is destruction of the quality of the land. The preferred solution for the advocates of this tale is private ownership of the resource in question so that the self-interest of each individual owner is to preserve and improve its productivity (in the case of the parable, the land, but also, among other resources, the buffalo herd, whales, fish, and presumably water and air). However, the focus upon the commons misidentifies and thus masks the tragedy. Rather than from common property, the concept of the tragedy of atomism reveals that the destruction of human beings and nature has its roots in particular social relations.

While the concept of the tragedy of atomism theoretically challenges the so-called tragedy of the commons, the latter has been refuted concretely by the history of communities with respect to common property. Focusing in particular on the experience with natural resources to which all members of a community have access (fisheries, irrigation systems, forests, and the like), many studies have stressed the norms, conventions, and working rules by which such communities, for example, indigenous communities, have successfully managed the commons.[3]

The key is the existence of communal institutions, formal or informal arrangements by which common property is monitored and respected. As Elinor Ostrom and others who have worked on the question of common property have explained, the absence of a community determined and able to monitor the utilization of the commons turns the latter into "open-access property." It means that there are no constraints upon atomistic behavior in which individuals, from inside or outside, act as if their private interests are isolated from one another. The result is excess grazing, fishing, hunting, land-clearing, chemical-fertilizing, mineral-extracting, carbon-emitting, water-using—excess relative to what Marx called "the whole gamut of permanent conditions of life required by the chain of human generations."[4]

Consistent with neoclassical theory, some communities avoid the tragedy of atomism by introducing sanctions and fines for violations of the interest of the whole; however, the constraint characteristic in many communities flows from the existence of norms with respect to fairness and appropriate behavior and morals. In contrast to the anonymous actors who populate neoclassical theory, individuals in these communities "have shared a past and expect to share a future. It is important," Elinor Ostrom accordingly notes, "for individuals to maintain their reputations as reliable members of the community."[5] In short, rather than a "connection of mutually indifferent persons," the links of people in such cases go beyond the atomistic premises of *homo economicus*.[6] Implicit here is a conception of fairness that goes beyond the results of markets.

"Fairness" and Experimental Economics

The concept of fairness (and, thus, unfairness) can be a real moment of economic life. As E. P. Thompson revealed in his classic article, "The Moral Economy of the English Crowd in the Eighteenth Century," the food riots of that period reflected a broad and passionate consensus that price increases were unfair and unjust.[7] Similarly, James Scott, in his work on "the moral economy of the peasant," focused upon the notion of economic justice among peasants and pointed to revolts and rebellions that erupted when notions of fairness were violated.[8] As I discussed in "The Concept of 'Fairness': Possibilities, Limitations, Possibilities," there were also protests and various forms of resistance within "real socialism" on the part of workers when what they considered to be tacit social contracts and existing norms were violated.[9]

The underlying concept here is one of an *equilibrium*, a concept that Thompson employed explicitly in talking about "a particular set of social relations, a particular equilibrium between paternalist authority and the crowd."[10] When that equilibrium is disturbed, there can be a feedback mechanism in which masses (peasants, the crowd, workers) react to restore the previous conditions. That was precisely what Marx described in *Value, Price and Profit*, where he pointed out that 99 percent of wage struggles followed changes that had produced falling wages. "In one word," he noted, they were "reactions of labour against the previous action of capital" and were an attempt to restore the "*traditional standard of life*" that was under attack.[11] The spontaneous impulse of workers was to struggle for "fairness" against the violations of existing norms, indeed, to fight a guerilla war against effects initiated by capital. The explicit goal of workers was to struggle for "a fair day's wage for a fair day's work."

This, as Marx pointed out, was a "conservative demand," an attempt to turn the clock back.[12] Rather than a call for an end to exploitation, it is the demand for the fair exploitation of the past. Indeed, the standard of fairness in much of what has been called "moral economy" involves looking backward to a better time. Is there not, though, a concept of fairness (and unfairness) that can lead in a revolutionary direction?

In recent years, the subject of fairness has surfaced in mainstream economics as the result of questions posed by experimental and behavioral economists about the neoclassical assumption of *homo economicus*. Through extensive empirical studies of select groups, supported by real life experiences, these economists and psychologists have concluded that predictions of that model are regularly falsified by the behavior of real subjects. Contrary to the premise that rational individuals by definition always act to maximize their personal self-interest, these writers argue that concepts of fairness are part of the preference functions of individuals and, accordingly, they act differently from *homo economicus*.

For example, Kahneman, Knetsch, and Thaler argue that the "Ultimatum Game," where one individual offers a particular division of a sum to a second individual on a "take-it-or leave-it basis" ("leave it" meaning that neither gets any part of that sum) reveals that people's preferences for being treated fairly and for treating others fairly lead them to act contrary to theoretical predictions. According to the theory, the first party (the allocator) rationally will offer as little above zero as possible and the second (the recipient) will accept this offer (ultimatum) rather than get nothing.[13] In this exercise a clear pattern emerges: the recipients often tend to reject any offer they don't consider fair even though this means they would get nothing, and the allocators often make an offer well above zero, and sometimes an equal division, rather than make a blatantly unfair offer.

An apparent preference for fairness is also demonstrated when those surveyed via telephone interviews and classroom tests consider a scenario in which an employer or landlord takes advantage of changing market conditions to alter an existing agreement (for example, raise rents or lower wages). Respondents tend to view such actions as unfair, except in the case where the employer/landlord himself faces additional costs. In contrast, new contracts with new parties that reflect those new conditions are viewed as fair. What leads the survey subjects to view the latter case as fair? The unstated premise is that the market yields fair results; as for the former case, the presumed unfairness flows from the violation of the implicit contract in a "reference transaction" that occurred under previous (and fair) market conditions.

Of course, the limited information these atomistic subjects are provided surely reflects their particular judgments as to fairness. If, for instance, they were informed that workers were super-exploited (in the reference transaction) as the result of racism and sexism, would they still conclude that it is fair for the employer to lower wages if his raw material costs rise? As Kahneman, Knetsch, and Thaler admit, justice is not to be confused with this conception of fairness: "The reference transaction provides a basis for fairness judgments because it is normal, not necessarily because it is just" and "Terms of exchange that are initially seen as unfair may in time acquire the status of a reference transaction."[14] As in the "moral economy" examples cited above, the concept of fairness here involves looking backward. In short, super-exploitation may come in time to be viewed as "self-evident natural laws."

Although the particular judgments of these survey respondents certainly may be questioned, a concept of fairness clearly appears to be part of their preference function. For Kahneman, Knetsch, and Thaler, incorporation of fairness enriches the standard model and helps to explain what appear to be anomalies for the model of *homo economicus*.[15] But does it challenge the standard neoclassical model? Fairness simply becomes here an additional element in the determination of the optimal position of atomistic individuals. A more realistic *homo economicus* that permits better predictions, perhaps, but still the same model.

Yet some behavioral economics studies point in a quite different direction, alerting us to contradictions between the self-interest characteristic of *homo economicus* and matters of fairness, morals, or what economist Sam Bowles calls "social preferences." In his book *The Moral Economy* Bowles defines social preferences as encompassing "motives such as altruism, reciprocity, intrinsic pleasure in helping others, aversion to inequity, ethical commitment, and other motives that induce people to help others more than is consistent with maxi-mizing their own wealth or material payoff."[16] Not only do many studies demonstrate that self-interest and social preferences coex-ist, but they also reveal particular characteristics of their interaction. Bowles illustrates this phenomenon at the outset of his book:

> In Haifa, at six day care centers, a fine was imposed on parents who were late in picking up their children at the end of the day. It did not work. Parents responded to the fine by doubling the fraction of time they arrived late. After twelve weeks, the fine was revoked, but the parents' enhanced tardiness persisted.[17]

Similarly, Bowles notes that Boston firemen responded to penalties for going over a limit for their sick days by substantially increasing the sick days they claimed and ultimately taking more than twice as many in the next year. Further, he points out that attempts to shorten hospital stays in Norway by imposing fines had the opposite effect. Contrary, then, to the predictions as to how *homo economicus* acts, the effect of monetary incentives in these cases appears counterintuitive.

But Bowles's point is that they are not anomalies. When you introduce concrete rewards or penalties where they are not hitherto present, something is occurring that the theory of *homo economicus* is not capturing. We can see that too in experiments with children who are offered a reward for doing what they were happy to do without the reward; for example, in the case of children happy to help an adult retrieve a lost object, with the introduction of a reward "the helping rate fell off by 40 percent." In another case where children enjoyed drawing, those who accepted the idea of rewards reduced their deci-sion to choose drawing in the course of time.[18]

We can identify two takeaways from these examples, and from the many experiments that Bowles reports. First, "incentives crowd out social preferences." We cannot assume, as the literature on *homo economicus* does, the compartmentalization or separation of the two spheres. Rather, "incentives and social preferences are substitutes: the effect of each on the targeted activity declines as the level of the other increases."[19] Thus, the fine for tardiness at the childcare center "appears to have undermined the parents' sense of ethical obligation to avoid inconveniencing the teachers, leading them to think of lateness as just another commodity they could purchase," and the fines placed on the Boston firemen went counter to their pride in serving the public.[20]

The second takeaway from Bowles's review of the various studies demonstrates the importance of the second product. Our emphasis upon the second product predicts that acting in response to material incentives tends to produce a different person than one who acts in accordance with social preferences. And that is precisely the lesson stressed by Bowles. Considering the long-term effects of material incentives, Bowles argues that "the economy is a great teacher, and its lessons are neither fleeting nor confined within its boundaries." Material incentives, he proposes, may "affect the long-term learning process whose results persist over decades, even entire lifetimes." Indeed, "the incentive alters the long term, not easily reversed preference-learning process." Very simply, "economies structured by differing incentives are likely to produce people with differing preferences," or, as Bowles declares in a subhead, "The Economy Produces People."[21]

What kinds of people are produced by the use of material incentives? Exactly what you would expect as the result of what Bowles calls "the corrosive effect of markets and incentives on social preferences."[22] Not only do incentives "crowd out" social preferences in the short run, but they also "constitute part of a learning environment in which preferences are durably modified."[23] More than mere substitutes for social preferences, material incentives shape people. As a result, the people produced by markets and incentives are substitutes for people characterized by motives such as altruism, opposition to inequity, and intrinsic pleasure in helping others. How Bowles feels about this is clear from the subtitle of his book: *Why Good Incentives Are No Substitute for Good Citizens.*

Nevertheless, despite his own obvious social preferences, Bowles sees the necessity to utilize material incentives in the hope of achieving desirable goals. Perhaps because of his understanding of how markets and material incentives have already shaped the preferences of people within capitalism, his purpose is to stress the importance of developing "public policies that would allow incentives and constraints to work synergistically rather than at cross purposes with people's ethical and other-regarding dispositions."[24] Rather than compromising the "ethical and other-regarding motives that are essential to a well-governed society," Bowles hopes for the development of a mechanism design that would include "a wise combination of positive incentives and punishments with moral lessons."[25] Combining incentives and social preferences in a way that fosters the latter would be for him the best of all possible worlds.

Having identified the essential contradiction between material incentives and social preferences, however, it is not enough to search for the golden mean, the "wise combination" that can dampen that contradiction and can offer an incremental feasible path toward a society that would produce better people. We can't stop there. If material incentives and social preferences are so obviously in opposition, it is because they are *elements of two different organic systems*. Analytically, we need to go beneath the surface to understand those systems that not only coexist but also interpenetrate and mutually deform each other.

Capitalism and Community

Material incentives are common sense in a system that starts from a relation of separated atomistic self-seekers, a system based not upon "the association of man with man, but on the separation of man from man."[26] What brings these "mutually indifferent persons" together, "putting them in relation with each other, is the selfishness, and the private interest of each. Each pays heed to himself only, and no one worries about the others."[27] Such atomistic self-seekers and their connection, the market, are "historic premises" of capitalism. Central to capitalism, however, is that it produces and reproduces a particular atomism, that of workers, as its premise.[28]

Consider our discussion in chapter 3 of capitalism as an organic system. Once capital has developed upon its own foundation (once "it is itself presupposed, and proceeds from itself to create the conditions of its maintenance and growth"), it produces its own premises in their "bourgeois economic form."[29] Commodities, money, markets, labor-power as a commodity, and the separation of workers are produced and reproduced as are the seemingly independent self-seekers who respond to the compulsion of the market, which is "external to the individuals and independent of them." That apparent external compulsion, which ensures the reproduction of capitalism as an organic system, is precisely why Marx stressed the importance of the "sacred" law of supply and demand in maintaining the despotism of capital and why he identified the political economy of capital as grounded in "the blind rule of the supply and demand laws."

Let us consider, on the other hand, the system that produces individuals who collectively are guided by "motives such as altruism, reciprocity, intrinsic pleasure in helping others, aversion to inequity, ethical commitment, and other motives that induce people to help others." In contrast to a concept of fairness that rests upon the market and only rejects as unfair those violations of existing norms developed as the result of the interactions of atomistic actors, focus upon social preferences implies the view that selfishness, inequality, and insensitivity to the needs of others are unfair and unjust behavior for people within society. We are pointing here to an alternative organic system in which social preferences are common sense. As Ostrom indicated, in a system based explicitly upon the association of people, people take pride in being viewed "as reliable members of the community." Whether labeled the solidarian society, the solidarity economy, the communal society, or communism, the starting point of this system is community, the recognition of the needs of others within society.[30]

Begin with communality, Marx proposed, and "instead of a division of labour . . . there would take place an organization of labour." There, the producers, "working with the means of production held in common," combine their capacities "in full self-awareness as one single social labour force."[31] In this system, Marx explained in the *Grundrisse*, "communal production, communality, is presupposed as the basis of production," and the activities undertaken by the associated producers are "determined by communal needs and communal purposes."[32] In short, here the producers have informed themselves of their common interests and accordingly "act in common."

In this system of communality, rather than "the blind rule of the supply and demand laws" inherent in the atomism of producers, we see the realization of "the political economy of the working class," which is "social production controlled by social foresight." Production for social needs, organized by associated workers, based upon social ownership of the means of production (three sides of what Hugo Chávez called "the elementary triangle of socialism") are parts of an organic system, a "structure in which all the elements coexist simultaneously and support one another." It is a system of reproduction whose results are premises of the system as "is the case with every organic system."[33]

One of the essential products of this system is a particular type of human being characterized by "solidarity, cooperation, care, reciprocity, mutualism, altruism, compassion, and love."[34] *Homo solidaricus* (as named by Emily Kawano) develops her capacities by relating to others out of solidarity. If I produce consciously for your need, the young Marx commented, I know my work is valuable: "in my individual activity," he proposed, "I would have directly *confirmed* and *realised* my true nature, my *human* nature, my *communal* nature." Thus, the second product of our activity in communal society is the development of rich human beings who realize themselves by consciously producing for others.[35] With "free exchange among individuals who are associated on the basis of common appropriation and control of the means of production," Marx envisioned the production of "free individuality, based on the universal development of individuals and on their subordination of their communal, social productivity as their social wealth."[36]

Two organic systems. Each is separate and compartmentalized. Each produces a particular type of human being. Actually existing capitalism contains elements of both systems, and that poses the question of how they interact. Bowles recognizes that incentives and social preferences are substitutes, that they tend to "crowd out" each other and that the people produced by each are substitutes. Given his chosen audience, he seeks to convince the wise legislator to search for the mechanism that will produce the most salutary combination of the two motives. But that does not abolish the contradictions between the two systems.

Capital, we know, is constantly attempting to separate producers in order to weaken them. It gains always by turning workers against each other and to see each other as competitors, as usurpers, as threats, as enemies. It does whatever it can to foster atomism and to turn everything into market relations; capital's goal in this respect is complete commodification, what Marx described as a "time when everything, moral or physical, having become a marketable value, is brought to the market," a time of "universal venality."[37] Capital, in short, constantly drives to crowd out all traces of the system of community. To think that a wise mechanism design is sufficient to withstand this impulse is utopianism.

Material incentive versus social preferences, atomism versus community, separation versus solidarity, *homo economicus* versus *homo solidaricus*, the political economy of capital versus the political economy of the working class—these are sides of the class struggle within existing capitalism.[38] Rather than hoping for "a wise combination" of each, the wise revolutionary understands that it is essential to struggle by all means possible to defeat capitalism, to decommodify everything, to build the system of community where producers act in common. And, simultaneously in that process, how they produce themselves as the working class the system of community needs.

9

Between Organic Systems

In chapter 3 we discussed Marx's conceptualization of capitalism as an organic system. There we see commodities, money, means of production, workers, all in their "bourgeois economic form," all as parts of a "structure of society in which all relations coexist simultaneously and support one another." This organic system, we understand, produces its own premises and, accordingly, is a system of reproduction: "Every economic relation presupposes every other in its bourgeois economic form, and everything posited is thus also a presupposition; this is the case with every organic system."[1]

Capitalism as an organic system would be a success story, one of capital's victory in subordinating all society to itself. The completion of an organic system, "its development to its totality," Marx indicated, "consists precisely in subordinating all elements of society to itself, or in creating out of it the organs which it still lacks. This is historically how it becomes a totality."[2] Here, capital no longer relies upon "historic premises"; its premises, including the working class that looks upon its requirements as common sense, are produced organically. It "proceeds from itself to create the conditions of its maintenance and growth."[3]

Actually existing capitalism, however, is not an organic system. As we have seen, existing capitalism contains elements that are alien to the organic system of capitalism, not only those social preferences that point directly to an alternative organic system of community but also the struggles and organization of workers who act in common to challenge "the blind rule of the supply and demand laws." Whereas capitalism as an organic system corresponds to the neoclassical ideal of atomistic actors functioning in a pure market system, actually existing capitalism contains elements of a different system, one in which "social production [is] controlled by social foresight."[4]

Lack of correspondence to the concept of an organic system is not unique for real capitalism. An organic system, by definition, is a particular combination of elements that produce and support one another and exist in harmony. However, in actual historical development, we find few such periods. Rather, as Hegel proposed, such periods are "blank pages" in history because "they are periods of harmony—periods when the antithesis is in abeyance."[5] On the contrary, the pages of history record a process of *becoming*, a process of struggle between old and new.

If organic systems have at best a fleeting real existence in which contradictions are suspended, it is reasonable to ask what is the point of focusing upon this concept? As we have seen, it is an intellectual construct that permits us to analyze a system in its purity and to identify its central premises. The concept of capitalism as an organic system allows us to identify the premises of capitalism that must be reproduced, namely capital and wage labor. How can we understand capitalism without recognizing how capital is reproduced and how wage labor is reproduced? Indeed, what is necessary for the reproduction of capitalist relations of production?

Further, as Marx noted, this method is a guide to historical investigation. Without identifying the premises of capitalism as an organic system, how do we know what to focus on in terms of the history of its emergence? With an understanding of those premises, we can read history backwards; we are able to ask where did capital initially come from and where did wage labor initially come from? But this guide is not only a guide to history; it is also a guide to revolutionary necessity.

That is, what is necessary to prevent those particular premises from being reproduced.

Contested Reproduction and the Whole

Given that existing capitalism contains elements that are alien to the organic system of capitalism, it is obvious that the latter is not the whole. Rather than a "structure of society in which all relations coexist simultaneously and support one another," existing capitalism contains elements that represent a potential rupture of that structure, a process of becoming that would negate capitalism. How, then, does a new system that is emerging subordinate all elements to itself, how does it wrest away from the old system those elements and create elements of its own? Conversely, how does the old system succeed in reproducing itself *despite* the inroads of the new? All history is a history of contested reproduction.

This concept of contested reproduction provides insight into the struggle over the state in the interregnum between the organic system of capitalism and the organic system of community. In capitalism as an organic system, there is no place for the state because the reproduction of capitalist relations occurs through the actions of atomistic capitals and atomistic workers, through, in short, the blind rule of the supply and demand laws. Similarly, in community as an organic system, there is no place for a state standing over and above civil society since the actions of associated self-governing communities and workplaces ensure the reproduction of communal relations. In contested reproduction between capitalism and community, however, the state is a site of struggle, to determine whether and to what extent it serves to support the reproduction of capitalism or the society of associated producers.

Within the whole that contains elements of capitalism and community, those parts do not merely coexist as independent and opposite. As indicated in chapter 2's discussion of parts and wholes, a dialectical worldview recognizes that parts interpenetrate. They "acquire properties by virtue of being parts of a particular whole, properties they do not have in isolation or as parts of another whole." In contested reproduction, the elements characteristic of particular organic systems are not present in their purity but are transformed by their interactions within the particular whole.

In both *The Socialist Alternative* and also *The Contradictions of "Real Socialism,"* I credited Evgeny Preobrazhensky as the theorist who made the most important contribution to an understanding of contested reproduction.[6] Preobrazhensky recognized that the becoming of a new organic system is a process of struggle in which the new must subordinate the elements of the old. "Not a single economic formation," he argued, "can develop in a pure form, on the basis merely of the immanent laws which are inherent to the particular formation. This would be in contradiction to the very idea of development. The development of any economic form means its ousting of other economic forms, the subordination of these forms to the new form, and their gradual elimination."[7] This is how the "pure" system, the new organic system, develops.

Discussing the particular challenges in the USSR in the 1920s, Preobrazhensky argued that that there was a "struggle between two mutually hostile systems" and, accordingly, a struggle between their regulating principles. On the one hand, there was "the law of the spontaneous equilibrium of commodity-capitalist society" (the law of value); on the other hand, there was the "law of primitive socialist accumulation" that involved "the conscious decisions of the regulatory organs of the state."[8] Each of these regulating principles reflected particular relations of production and pointed to a particular organic system. "If each principle is fighting for supremacy in the whole system," he noted, "it is thereby fighting for the type of regulation which is organically characteristic of the particular system of production-relations, taken in its pure form."[9]

Yet, neither the law of value nor that of primitive socialist accumulation regulated the Soviet economy in this period. Rather, Preobrazhensky argued, the two regulating principles interpenetrated—coexisting, limiting, deforming each other—and their combination generated dysfunction in the economy.[10] If the regulating principle of primitive socialist accumulation existed by itself, the pattern in the Soviet economy would be rapid accumulation in the sphere of heavy industry (Department I) because of the need for mechanization and rapid industrialization.[11] On the other hand, if only the regulating principle of the law of value were present in its pure form, then the free movement of prices and of capital between different branches of production would direct production to light industry in order to satisfy consumer demand.[12] With the combination of the two principles (one tending to foster the growth of Department II and the other the growth of Department I), the result was the emergence of a "goods famine," a "disproportion between industrial production and the country's effective demand."

In this situation, Preobrazhensky argued, the operation of the law of value was "quite deformed and distorted" because it could not produce the distribution of the country's productive forces consistent with it.[13] On the other hand, the attempt to plan and coordinate the state economy was subject to "continual blows struck by market spontaneity against the entire state economy as a unified whole."[14] The problem was that the old was dying but the new could not yet be born. It is the consequence of a "situation when the working of one fundamental law, in this case the law of value, is paralysed or, to speak more precisely, is half-abolished, but the working of the other law, which historically succeeds the law of value, cannot develop for one reason or another proportionately to the stage and rate of abolition of the law of value."[15]

Who will win? In contested reproduction, the outcome of the struggle to subordinate the elements of each other is not predetermined. In the case of the Soviet Union, Preobrazhensky stated that "the enormous preponderance of petty commodity production combined with the relative weakness of the state sector forces the state economy into an uninterrupted economic war with the tendencies of capitalist development, with the tendencies of capitalist restoration."[16] For socialism to advance, he argued that it was essential that primitive socialist accumulation replace the law of value, that the latter be subordinated and gradually eliminated.

The whole that Preobrazhensky described, in short, contained within it the struggle between two systems.[17] And, characteristic of wholes marked by contested reproduction, there is always the possibility that neither system will prevail over the other for significant periods of time. Accordingly, stability and equilibrium, that is, homeostasis, will appear to characterize the whole. Even when—indeed, *especially* when—the whole appears stable, it is essential to recognize that the whole contains opposing forces, that it is characterized by contested reproduction. As Levins and Lewontin noted, in such cases, "Things are the way they are because of the temporary balance of opposing forces."[18]

The Strength of Opposing Forces

Marx certainly understood the concept of contested reproduction. "Two diametrically opposed economic systems," Marx proposed in *Capital*, coexisted and were in contradiction. One, he noted, "rests on the labour of the producer himself, and the other on the exploitation of the labour of others." What distinguished those diametrically opposed systems was the beneficiary of the producer's labor. In the first, the producer, "as owner of his own conditions of labour, employs that labour to enrich himself instead of the capitalist."[19] In the second, capital grows by exploiting workers.

Contested reproduction in this case was thus characterized by the attempt of capital to subordinate the elements of the system of producer-owned production and the attempt of that system to resist and reverse any inroads made by capital. Of course, this was a process and not something that occurred overnight. It involved many intermediate steps before the victory of capitalist relations of production (the relation of capitalist and wage-labor) could be complete: "The process, therefore, which creates the capital-relation can be nothing other than the process which divorces the worker from the ownership of the conditions of his own labour."[20] This was the victory of one economic system.

Viewed from the other side, separation of producer and conditions of production represented the destruction of the system of producer-owned production. "Where the worker is the free proprietor of the conditions of his labour, and sets them in motion himself: where the peasant owns the land he cultivates, or the artisan owns the tools with which he is an accomplished performer," a particular mode of production, small-scale production, "flourishes, unleashes the whole of its energy, attains its adequate classical form." In place, accordingly, of a system that permitted "the free individuality of the worker himself," there emerged the system that destroyed producers. [21]

How in general did capital make inroads into the system of producer-owned production? Through *money*, by successively subordinating every element of the existing system to money, the germ of capital. As Marxist historian Jairus Banaji stressed, independent producers often were increasingly subordinated to capital as the result of bad harvests and growing difficulties in reproducing themselves and their conditions of production. In this situation, interest-bearing loans, advances, and the putting-out of raw materials were means by which money-capital and merchant-capital came to dominate those independent producers.[22] From selling their products in order to buy particular use-values to selling commodities to secure money to repay debts, those producers were increasingly driven by the market rather than by their reproduction requirements.

Yet bad years could be succeeded by good years and low commodity prices by high prices. And, in those latter circumstances, producers could extract themselves from dependence upon capital. Those producers, after all, were the owners of their output and the immediate beneficiaries of their own labor. As residual claimants of the returns from their production, in good years they were able to pay off debts and avoid incurring new ones. Indeed, insofar as they produced to maintain their families (effectively a fixed cost), high prices for their output reduced the necessity to sell and could be accompanied by reduced marketing. These independent producers were not capitalist firms.

Even when the inroads made by money-capital extended to the point where producers were separated from the conditions of production, and it was capitalist employers who were now the residual claimants of production, producers struggled to extract themselves from wage-labor. Indeed, as Marx pointed out, "centuries are required before the 'free' worker . . . makes a voluntary agreement" to sell "the whole of his active life, his capacity for labour in return for the price of his cus-tomary means of subsistence."[23] Accordingly, as noted earlier, in "the historical genesis of capitalist production," accumulation of capital drove up money-wages; where possible, this allowed workers to meet their monetary requirements and to spend more time on other activ-ity. Negative feedback following the growth of capital at such times tended to generate the non-reproduction of the wage-labor relation.[24] And that is precisely why capital drew upon the state through "bloody discipline," "police methods," and "state compulsion" to ensure the submission of workers to the needs of capital.[25]

Though this negative feedback that tended to check the reproduc-tion of capitalism was present in the Old World, nowhere was it more obvious than in the New World, the "colonies." There, the high wages generated by the accumulation of capital provided an opportunity for workers to *save* in order to extract themselves from wage labor. As a result, Marx explained, "Today's wage-labourer is tomorrow's independent peasant or artisan, working for himself." In short, in the colonies the relative supply and demand for workers meant that the relationship of wage labor was not automatically reproduced: where "the worker receives more than is required for the reproduction of his labour capacity and very soon becomes a peasant farming indepen-dently, etc., the original relation is not constantly reproduced."[26] And that meant that the reproduction of capital was threatened because the reproduction of the worker as wage laborer "is the absolutely neces-sary condition for capitalist production."[27] The answer to this problem, accordingly, was state legislation to impose a price upon land (as pre-scribed by E. G. Wakefield, the English theorist of colonization). Here was "the secret discovered in the New World by the political economy of the Old World"—capitalism has as its "fundamental condition the annihilation of that private property which rests on the labour of the individual himself; in other words, the expropriation of the worker."[28]

Contested Reproduction and One-Sidedness

Every whole is characterized by "diametrically opposed economic systems" whose relative force is contingent upon particular concrete conditions. In the struggle between producer-owned and capitalist-owned productive forces, for example, the strength of each may vary between time, place, and particular sectors. This was the case of the contrast between the Old World and the New World with respect to the force of the respective systems. So, too, with the relative strength of opposing forces between peasant agriculture and state-directed industry during NEP and in the struggle between capitalism and community now—all are affected by concrete circumstances.

When there is contested reproduction, how do we classify the whole? As the new struggling to be born or as the old struggling to be reproduced? Unfortunately, there is a tendency to consider the struggle between systems one-sidedly. This tendency is present when contested reproduction is equated with the concept of transition. In place of a concept of "becoming" (which encompasses both an arising and a declining), "transition" introduces more than a hint of teleology—the presupposed victory of the new. Further, it can lead to the view of historical development as the result of "the immanent laws which are inherent to the particular formation."

Contested reproduction between capitalist and pre-capitalist relations of production is particularly susceptible to a view of the whole from the side of capital. Banaji, for example, explicitly classifies slave plantations, sharecropping, putting out systems, Indian and Russian peasant agriculture, etc., as capitalist production even though they lack the *differentia specifica* of capitalist production, namely, exploitation of wage-laborers by capitalists.[29] But that is his central point, that it is an *error*, "bad theory," to define capitalist relations of production by the exploitation of wage-laborers. Wage-labor, he insists, "*cannot* be an essential moment of capital, not if the self-expansion of value is intrinsically indifferent to the forms in which it dominates labour.[30]" Indeed, for Banaji, "the naïve conception of 'relations of production' as forms of exploitation of labour" retains characteristics of "vulgar historical materialism," and "the ossified pseudo-Marxism of the Stalinists."[31]

Given Marx's consistency in describing capitalist relations of production ("the capital-relation") as the production relation between capitalist and wage-laborer, and given his understanding that "what distinguishes the various economic formations of society—the distinction between for example a society based on slave labour and a society based on wage labour—is the form in which the surplus labour is in each case extorted from the immediate producer, the worker," then it should be obvious that, by insisting that we must not identify "the specific economic form in which unpaid surplus labor is pumped out of the direct producers" with relations of production, Banaji's critique is not of "ossified pseudo-Marxism" but of Marx himself.[32]

But how does this difference with Marx come about? Very simply, because Banaji's definition of capitalist relations of production does not include capitalist *production*. Rather, he delimits capitalist relations of production to M-C-M', the impulse of capital to grow: "the self-expansion of capital," "the accumulation of capital," "the accumulation and competition of capitals."[33] With this truncated definition, he has the degree of freedom sufficient to declare capitalist relations of production compatible with peasant communities, slavery, feudalism, and a wide range of forms of exploitation. Banaji thus assures us, "Relations of production are simply not reducible to forms of exploitation." In particular, once merchant-capital and money-capital are able to extract surplus value from various forms of production, he argues that the latter should be understood as differing forms of exploitation under capitalist relations.[34]

Given Banaji's determination to explore the role of merchant-capital and money-capital in what have been traditionally viewed as pre-capitalist relations of production, he has contributed considerable insights into the nature of those social formations. Indeed, much of his impressive literature survey and commentary demonstrates the existence of contested reproduction throughout the ages. But not for Banaji. Unfortunately, contested reproduction between capitalism and pre-capitalism is present in his work *only negatively and one-sidedly*. It is revealed in barriers to the *ought* of capital, barriers that are the result of "feudally dominated habits of consumption and display" (slave plantations), "the social-consumption needs of the owners" (feudalism), and "the patriarchal logic of the subsistence mode of production" (peasant-economy). It's all capitalism, despite the "relatively slow and mainly sporadic" advance where the labor process is not determined and ruled by capital.[35]

Absent a focus upon contested reproduction as two-sided, Banaji offers a picture of a long march through transitional forms of capitalism, a long stage of "commercial capitalism" that encompasses centuries of the relations of money-capital with differing forms of exploitation. In place of the old schema of slavery, feudalism, capitalism, he describes "initial stages of capitalism," extending from the twelfth to the late eighteenth centuries. Here, "the history of commercial capitalism is no longer simply a prelude to industrial capital"; rather, it is "best seen as a *totality*, a narrative with its own coherence, forms, internal periodisation, and conceptions of empire."[36] In his theoretical reading, "the immanent laws which are inherent to the particular formation" explains the history of capitalism.

Commercial capitalism is, indeed, distinct from the organic system of capitalism that Marx analyzed, one in which merchant and money capital were subordinate to the results of capitalist exploitation. By contrast, in Banaji's whole, "circulation dominates production," and commercial capitalism develops as the result of its immanent laws. Lost is the understanding of Preobrazhensky (to whom Banaji dedicated his book) that the process of development involves the "struggle between two mutually hostile systems."[37]

Classification and Change

Classification often brings with it the tendency to emphasize the static characteristics of one particular organic system within the whole. For example, is today's China capitalist, socialist, or producer-owned peasant production? Was the "Pink Tide" in Latin America capitalist,

twenty-first century socialist or something else? And how to classify
the Soviet NEP period and Yugoslav self-management?

In contrast, the concept of contested reproduction guides us to
focus upon the process of *becoming*, a process of struggle in which
each system is attempting to subordinate the other. Accordingly,
rather than planting our flag on one or another static category, we
examine a whole *in motion*. We are stimulated to evaluate every event
or policy as strengthening or weakening one or another system. What
was the effect, for example, of the Civil War upon potentially contest-
ing systems in the Soviet Union? Or the effect of imperialist actions or
global capitalism upon the correlation of forces in China, Vietnam, or
Venezuela? What logic is strengthened by current reforms in Cuba?[38]

Focusing upon contested reproduction, however, does not exclude
the need to identify the dominant characteristics of a society at a
given time. Without assuming that any particular point is static and
frozen, as Marxists we ask what *"specific economic form" of exploitation (or non-exploitation) of the direct producers* dominates? As noted
above, for Marx, what distinguished societies (for example between
one based on slavery and one based upon wage labor) was "the form
in which the surplus labour is in each case extorted from the immediate producer, the worker." Accordingly, when we describe a system
as capitalism, we mean that capitalist exploitation of wage laborers is
dominant within this whole marked by contested reproduction.

But that brings us back to Banaji, who rejects a distinction between
economic formations based upon forms of exploitation. Since in his
whole, capitalist circulation dominates production, he gets everything
backwards. Rather than privileging capitalist circulation, from Marx's
perspective, the exploitation of the slave is the premise for the circulation of money capital (as is the exploitation of the serf). Privileging
capitalist circulation obscures the differences between "the various
economic formations of society."

On the other hand, if we classify the whole *simply* as slavery or feudalism, respectively, we miss the importance of the interaction with
money-capital in each case and the ensuing process of change. That is
the problem with classification, and it is the rational core of Banaji's

critique. The motion and change characteristic of contested reproduction are not easily captured by classification.

Perhaps this is why Levins and Lewontin propose that, as Marxists,
there are two separate questions. One, discussed in chapter 2, relates to
the reproduction of a system that contains interacting and interpen-
etrating parts. We speak of homeostasis in this case when the system
is characterized by a balance of opposing forces, when the generation
of positive and negative feedback tends to produce an equilibrium
state. We understand that whole by analyzing how its parts interact.
In this context, we ask what are the various forms of exploitation,
what is their relative size and strength within the whole, and how they
interact. This is the matter addressed by their first question, why are
things the way they are.

The second question focuses upon how things change, how things
get the way they are; this is the question that considers development,
evolution, and the non-equilibrium processes that tend to produce
qualitative change in systems. It is this second question that concerns
us for our discussion of contested reproduction, and it is where we
need to be sensitive to the problem of one-sidedness. In the struggle
between old and new, if you focus only upon the new (by stressing,
for example, the effect of the growth of money-capital within pre-
capitalist formations), then the story told is one of *inroads* which the
new makes into the old, the encroachment that produces a growing
subordination of the elements of the old.

On the other hand, if the side of the old is the starting point, we
can see that changes in the whole may be initiated by changes within
the old—for example, where negative feedbacks that fostered homeostasis are weakened or reverse their sign entirely and become positive
feedbacks.[39] Such factors as soil erosion, declining sources of slave
supplies, invasions, climate change, overpopulation (relative to the
supply of land), economic crises, war, as well as state actions, may
tend to produce disequilibrium in the existing system. In those cases,
rather than inroads into the old, we focus upon *openings* produced
by changes within the old that are the immediate source of potential
qualitative changes of the whole.

Between organic systems, openings and inroads interact, just as the old and new do in the process of contested reproduction. How that can allow the new society to subordinate the elements of the old, in particular, how the system of community can subordinate capitalism, remains to be explored.

10

How to Find a Path to Community

Writing History Backwards

How can we understand the process by which a new system emerges? In his essay "When Should History Be Written Backwards?" economist Wassily Leontiev argued that the appropriate approach to writing "analytical history" is determined by the equilibrium properties of the particular dynamic system in question.[1] If there is a stable dynamic system, the trajectory of the system will be insensitive to a particular starting point because the tendency in any event will be for the system to converge at a given equilibrium point. Accordingly, writing history forward, following chronological time, is unproblematic in this case because differing historical observations at the starting point will not affect the ultimate outcome.

In contrast, with an unstable dynamic system, the starting point is critical as a slight difference at the outset will produce significantly divergent historical outcomes. "A small, hardly perceptible mistake in the description of the original base-year position of an unstable dynamic system is bound to bring about a major error in the prediction, that is, explanation of its later states." Accordingly, "A historian who sets out to explain the development of such a system by tracing the sequence of events in time," Leontiev commented, "is indeed embarking on a very exacting, not to say practically impossible, enterprise."[2] Where there is an unstable dynamic system, we should begin from the known in the present and to write analytical history backwards "with the help of theoretical weapons step by step toward the more and more distant path."[3]

Although not focusing upon the dynamic properties of systems, philosopher Bertell Ollman comes to the same conclusion because of his understanding of dialectics. In "Why Dialectics?" Ollman argued that the correct order of inquiry with respect to history is to begin with the present, not the past. With that starting point, he argued, we can decide what to look for as well as how far back to go in looking for it. In that way, we ask "what had to happen in the past for the present to become what it did."[4] Ollman expanded on this point in an essay specially focused upon writing history backwards: "Necessity read backward into the past is of an altogether different order than the necessity that begins in the past and follows a predetermined path into the future."[5]

If the dynamic properties of a system are such that the historical process is one in which a germ is necessarily realized over time, then writing history forward would be appropriate. "Directionality" here is built in, and following from that, Levins and Lewontin comment, is "a succession of ordered phases through which each entity must pass, the successful passage through one stage being the condition for passing on to the next."[6] However, if the combination of parts and the re-creation of both parts and whole through their interaction makes the historical trajectory of the whole highly sensitive to those interactions, then how can there be "a predetermined path into the future"? As Victor Serge commented, in the Soviet Union there were *many* germs. Where there is contested reproduction (that is, class struggle between systems), no outcome is inevitable.

In *Capital,* history was written forward (without teleological necessity) *once the elements of the capital relation were assembled.* Having set out the capital relation, Marx traced the trajectory of capital as it attempted to drive beyond all barriers to its growth in the context of contested reproduction. However, he did not write history forward in order to identify the original emergence of the essential premises of capitalism, capital, and wage-labor. He did not analyze feudalism in order to explain how its disintegration and decomposition created the elements for the construction of capitalism. Given the multiplicity of elements present at the time when feudal relations imploded, how could anyone identify the "historic premises" of capitalism without first understanding capitalism?

As we have seen, Marx's analysis of capitalism as a stable system of reproduction was the condition for reading necessity "backward into the past." By writing history backwards from the known present, Marx developed a method by which we are able to identify, despite the vast differences of experiences in different countries, what led to capitalism in each case. That method, we saw in chapter 3, "indicates the points where historical investigation must enter in"; understanding the nature of capitalism as an organic system "point[s] towards a past lying behind this system."[7]

Imagine, though, that we began with the contradictions of feudalism in Western Europe and attempted to write history forward. How could we identify a path to capitalism as opposed to something else? Historical paths are inherently unstable; given the sensitivity of outcomes to the interaction of parts and wholes, any slight deviation in the starting point (for example, the disintegration of feudalism) might lead to someplace other than capitalism. The point is critical. If you write history forward, how can you understand the *next* system? If capitalism disintegrates, what system emerges in its place?

There's no problem if teleology trumps dialectics. Then, history follows that "predetermined path into the future." Slavery begets feudalism, which begets capitalism, which begets socialism, which begets communism. It is all inevitable, sooner or later. From a dialectical standpoint, however, things are not so simple. Once we understand that change is the result of the interaction of parts and wholes and that particular events and interactions, internal or external, may produce quite divergent outcomes, we acknowledge that there is no royal road to the future.

The problematic relation between the disintegration of feudalism and the emergence of capitalism is reproduced if we consider contested reproduction between the organic system of capitalism and the organic system of community. If we write history forwards, it is assumed that the contradictions of capitalism that we have analyzed are sufficient to yield the movement to community. But are they?

History from Capitalism to Community

With the development of the contradictions of capitalism, there are openings and inroads with potential for going beyond capitalism. In chapter 4 we saw that capitalism creates regular openings through its periodic short-term and long-term crises. It is, in short, constantly put on trial by its inherent tendencies for crisis. However, in capitalism as an organic system those openings in the form of crises tend to be self-correcting, not simply because of the negative feedbacks generated by particular crises but because of the nature of the working class that capital produces, a working class that looks upon the needs of capitalism as self-evident natural laws. Given the second product of capital, crises in and of themselves are not sufficient to lead in the direction of a new system.

Here, however, we are not considering capitalism as an organic system. Rather, before us is a whole that contains elements that are from outside that organic system. We have seen, for example, how struggles of the working class over the workday transformed workers. They come out of such struggles, victorious or not, more conscious of their strength, as their own second products with the potential of becoming "the self-conscious, independent movement of the immense majority, in the interest of the immense majority."[8]

Accordingly, it is possible that workers who have developed their capacities and instruments for struggle will not only respond to capitalism's crises by taking advantage of those openings but will make inroads into capitalism on their own. If we consider only the side of workers, we see in the *Communist Manifesto* that once the working class is successful in winning "the battle of democracy," it will use "its political supremacy to wrest, by degrees, all capital from the bourgeoisie." Of course, it cannot do this all at once. "Despotic inroads on the right of property, and on the conditions of bourgeois production" are not in themselves sufficient but, as the movement proceeds, would "outstrip themselves, [and] necessitate further inroads upon the old social order."[9]

It must not be forgotten, though, that capital is still there, and it does not passively allow for such inroads to be made. Capital resists. It treats all inroads as barriers to its own growth, barriers that must be transcended. We are one-sided if we forget that we are talking about capitalism in contested reproduction. When a working-class government takes measures that make inroads into capitalist reproduction, capital goes on strike. It ceases investment and/or moves elsewhere where such inroads are not occurring. The results can be crises, crises as a response to inroads, and a government that has been elected to advance the interests of the working class under these circumstances may retreat. As noted in chapter 4, what Lukács called the "immaturity of the proletariat" may mean that capital continues to lead the way out of crises.

However, let's assume that the government does not retreat but seizes the opportunity given by capitalist reaction to make "further inroads upon the old social order." How does this lead to community rather than to something else? Is the disarticulation of the elements of capitalism sufficient to produce the particular combination characteristic of the organic system of community? Or will the result be state capitalism, market self-management of socially owned enterprises, a system based upon vanguard relations of production, or something else? Precisely which elements of capitalism must the system of community subordinate and what, if any, new organs must it create? Writing history forward fails at the very point when we want to consider the passage from one system to another.

Writing History Backwards from the Future

If we write history backwards, on the other hand, we would be asserting that the characteristics of community permit us to identify what must be subordinated for the system of community to emerge, or, paraphrasing Ollman, what has to happen in the present for the future to become what it must. Of course, the system of community is not the known present from which we can read backwards. But does the method nevertheless permit us to gain insight into the path to community?

Yes, Marx answered. There is no better example of writing history backwards from a possible future than Marx's *Critique of the Gotha Programme*. The future described there is "a communist society . . . as it has *developed* on its own foundations." In this society where "the instruments of labour are common property and the total labour is co-operatively regulated," the basis of production is what Marx called "communal production, communality," where production is "determined by communal needs and communal purposes." In this "completed" society that produces its own premises, the "all-round development of the individual"—based upon ending "the enslaving subordination of the individual to the division of labour" and "the antithesis between mental and physical labour"—ensures that "all the springs of cooperative wealth flow more abundantly." The organic system of community is here complete.

Of course, this new system, like all systems, does not emerge fully developed from the preceding one. It does not immediately produce its own premises but is dependent upon "historic premises," elements from the old system, elements that it must subordinate in order to stand upon its own foundations. Even though the working class may have successfully wrested "all capital from the bourgeoisie" and centralized "all instruments of production in the hands of the State," the new system as it emerges is necessarily defective. It is "in every respect, economically, morally, and intellectually, still stamped with the birthmarks of the old society from whose womb it emerges."

Consider those birthmarks. One defect that Marx explicitly identified was the continuation of "bourgeois right." Despite common ownership of the means of production, private ownership of labor-power brings with it the insistence upon an exchange in which the producer is entitled to an equivalent for his own individual labor.[10] As

Marx stressed, this emphasis upon exchange of equivalents (subsequently labelled "the socialist principle") produces inequality, in that the individual owner of labor power considers "unequal individual endowment and thus productive capacity as natural privileges." Not only is this a source of inequality, but this birthmark of the old society infects the development of the new society. The combination of private ownership of labor-power and common ownership of the means of production brings with it dysfunctional tendencies.

If the individual producer is entitled to an equivalent for his present labor, why not for his *past* labor (an obvious phenomenon in the case of Yugoslav self-management)? And if the producer does not consider that the equivalent he is offered is a true equivalent, to what extent would he offer less labor, thus, lower his contribution? Or to what extent might he engage in theft of the means of production in order to increase his own income (to "get his own back")? The self-interest that flows from the private ownership of labor-power constantly undermines the new society.

That is why bourgeois right must be subordinated. Unfortunately, generations of Marx's disciples have distorted his explanation of how the new society can succeed in subordinating the elements of the old. Rather than writing history backwards from the fully developed system, they have insisted on *building* upon the new society's defects. In this whole marked by contested reproduction, insistence upon the "socialist principle" is the ideological weapon that tilts the whole back in the direction of capitalism. Indeed, whenever contradictions in the emerging society produce crises, that principle has been invoked from above to fight against the concepts of community. "Serious infractions of the socialist principle of distribution according to work," in Mikhail Gorbachev's words, are blamed for the egalitarianism and leveling that prevent private initiative and advance.[11] Behind "reforms" determined to free the "socialist principle" lurks the specter of capitalism.

Marx, however, did not make this mistake. Starting from his conception of the communist society developed upon its own foundations, he identified what was necessary to subordinate the inherited defects from the old society. At the very outset of his *Critique*, he pointed to two immediate changes that occur in the new society and that develop further "in proportion as the new society develops." Those two changes are introduced in his discussion of deductions from the total product of labor, deductions to be made before there is to be any consideration of distribution of the residual among individuals. One deduction concerns production "*intended for the common satisfaction of needs*." "From the outset," Marx insisted, "this part grows considerably in comparison with present-day society, and it grows in proportion as the new society develops."

So, *from the outset*, a new principle of distribution begins to crowd out the old. There is increased production for the commons and a diminishing residual for distribution in accordance with contribution. "What the producer is deprived of in his capacity as a private individual benefits him directly or indirectly in his capacity as a member of society." As the new society develops, we no longer regard the producers one-sidedly, that is, "*only as workers* and nothing more is seen in them, everything else being ignored." Rather, the producers are understood as a whole, as members of society.

There are other deductions from the total social product, and these include "replacement of means of production used up" and a "portion for expansion of production." Those deductions are "an economic necessity and their magnitude is to be determined according to available means and forces." But there was one other deduction particularly relevant to building the new society upon its own foundations, and that concerns the state—"*the general costs of administration not belonging to production*." That deduction would *fall*: "This part will, from the outset, be very considerably restricted in comparison with present-day society and it diminishes in proportion as the new society develops."

But why the "very considerably restricted" deduction for the state from the outset? Observation of subsequent socialist experiments would suggest precisely the *opposite* course, namely, growing bureaucracy and petty tutelage over all aspects of the society! For Marx, however, the point was self-evident. As he had learned from the

Paris Commune four years earlier, from the very outset, state functions are to be "wrested from an authority usurping pre-eminence over society itself and restored to the responsible agents of society."[12] If the Commune had succeeded, Marx proposed, in place of the old centralized government, "all France would have been organized into self-working and self-governing communes." And the result would be "state functions reduced to a few functions for general national purposes."[13] In the words of the *Critique*, the state would be converted more and more "from an organ superimposed upon society into one completely subordinate to it."

Underlying his stress upon a "very considerably restricted" state, Marx obviously had in mind a different kind of state, one that involved new organs, those self-working and self-governing communes. As the new system developed, gone would be another defect—the old state inherited from capitalism with its "systematic and hierarchic division of labour" and where state administration and governing are treated as "mysteries, transcendent functions only to be trusted to the hands of a trained caste—state parasites, richly paid sycophants and sinecurists."[14] The new state from below, "the political form at last discovered under which to work out the economical emancipation of Labour," immediately makes despotic inroads and increasingly crowds out the old state as a measure of the development of the new society.[15]

Following Marx in writing history backwards from communism, we can identify what has to happen for the future to become what it must. As the new system develops, it must increasingly produce its own premises. By producing consciously for common needs and purposes and directing society through self-working and self-governing communes, the associated producers transform society and transform themselves. They produce communist society as it has developed on its own foundations.

But what if the system that emerges from capitalism, infected "in every respect, economically, morally, and intellectually," does not remove the defects it has inherited? If the system were dynamically stable such that any initial deviations nevertheless would converge, that clearly would not affect the preordained outcome. However, if the system is dynamically unstable, the failure to subordinate these defects leads to someplace else, and you cannot say where with any certainty if you are trying to write history forwards. Perhaps we can gain insights into the implications of the missing premises by writing history backwards from a different system, one often referred to as "real socialism."

Writing "Real Socialism" Backwards

In *Contradictions of "Real Socialism": The Conductor and the Conducted*, I attempted to analyze "real socialism" as a particular organic system, a system of reproduction that more or less consolidated in the second half of the twentieth century in several countries.[16] Though it contained elements of competing logics, characteristic of this system was, on the one hand, a particular form of state ownership and central planning permeated by enforced hierarchy in both the economy and social organizations, so that institutions functioned as transmission belts from the state. On the other hand, "real socialism" tended to provide workers with full employment, job security, free and widely accessible healthcare and education, subsidized necessities, and a relative degree of income equality.

Though these latter benefits were appreciated by workers, given their contrast to previous experiences and capitalist patterns of unemployment, insecurity, and deprivation of essential services, they came at a definite cost. Decisions in workplaces and society came from above, and attempts to organize from below or even to express publicly the desire to do so were viewed as threats to stability and harmony by those above and, accordingly, were marginalized and/ or penalized. This combination of benefits and prohibitions in "real socialism" may be considered a "social contract," although, as Boris Kagarlitsky explained, it was an "obligatory social contract" in that "the population was forced into it."[17] The result was an atomized yet secure working class that was not able to develop its capacities through its practice. Insofar as the benefits (to the extent they continued) were apparent and the costs of challenging the relation obvious, maintenance of this social contract ensured the reproduction of the system.

In the same way that Marx analyzed capital and wage-labor as the essential premises of capitalism, I identified the premise of "real socialism" as the vanguard party and its relation to the working class.[18] Characteristic of the vanguard party, I proposed, is a commitment to system change (replacing capitalism with socialism) and the insistence upon a disciplined, centralized party to achieve this goal.[19] I summed up the character of the vanguard party as follows:

> The goal of system change distinguishes the concept of the vanguard party from a body of self-interested bureaucrats or would-be capitalists. It begins from a clear rejection of capitalism and the belief in the necessity of socialism. Given that essential goal, the question is: What is to be done? Characteristic for the supporters of the vanguard party is the conviction that the achievement of this goal will not happen spontaneously; it requires leadership. The orchestra needs a conductor. And since the conductor alone can see the whole picture and has the whole score before him, there is no place for spontaneity and improvisation. Discipline and hierarchy are essential. Within the workplace and community, it is only appropriate that all parts, all instruments, follow a predetermined plan determined by the vanguard party. Socialism in this perspective is a gift to those below by those above, who are the only ones who know how to create socialism.[20]

There are two hierarchical relations here. One is the internal relation within the party. "Democratic centralism," in principle, ensures that there is the greatest possible democracy in arriving at decisions and the greatest possible centralization and discipline in executing those decisions. The two aspects, democracy and discipline, may vary in their weight in practice: democracy is often episodic, confined to party congresses and collective decision-making occasions, whereas discipline is meant to be part of daily life. The potential for imbalance is very high: those toward the top in the hierarchy may want confidence that their subordinates will carry out party policy faithfully; in this respect, rather than the bottom selecting the top, as democratic centralism would suggest, the top selects the bottom.[21] Implicit in the vanguard party are the acceptance of discipline and the reluctance to engage in "individualistic behavior," characteristics of internal party life within "real socialism."[22]

The other hierarchical relation is that between the party and society. The party takes on the role of educator to pupil, leader to the led, conductor to the conducted. From this perspective, social movements are considered below the party as such and are viewed as bodies from which to recruit potential party cadres and to subordinate to the party completely, as occurs especially in "real socialism." The presumed superiority of the party, following from its "banked knowledge" in the form of "Marxism-Leninism," gives it the license to work to change circumstances for people, irrespective of Marx's comment that such a doctrine divides "society into two parts, one part of which is superior to society."

Identification of the roots of "real socialism" with the vanguard party is not at all a critique of the role of any party in providing leadership to go beyond capitalism and to build the system of community. Consider a party instead that stresses the process by which people transform themselves and develop their capacities. Envision a party that rejects a focus upon delivering "banked knowledge" to the underlying population, one that rejects the conception, described by Paulo Freire, in which "knowledge is a gift bestowed by those who consider themselves knowledgeable upon those who they consider to know nothing."[23]

In contrast to the vanguard party, a party focused upon the centrality of the concept of revolutionary practice, that simultaneous changing of circumstance and self-change, is not likely to converge at "real socialism." As Leontiev argued, "A small, hardly perceptible mistake in the description of the original base-year position of an unstable dynamic system is bound to bring about a major error in the prediction, that is, explanation of its later states." The difference between the classic vanguard party and a party that is guided by the concept of the second product, though, is hardly small and imperceptible.

11

Taking a Path to Community

If you don't know where you want to go, no path will take you there. But we do know where we want to go. We want a society in which the relation between its members is guided by "motives such as altruism, reciprocity, intrinsic pleasure in helping others, aversion to inequity, ethical commitment, and other motives that induce people to help others." In communal society, the self-evident natural law for *homo solidaricus* would be that "the free development of each is the condition for the free development of all."[1] And that means we want a society based upon protagonism in all aspects of life and solidarity. In this society characterized by "free individuality, based on the universal development of individuals and on their subordination of their communal, social productivity as their social wealth," the producers combine their capacities "in full self-awareness as one single social labour force" and "all the springs of cooperative wealth flow more abundantly."

Premises of the System of Community

Communal society, like all organic systems, produces its own premises. As discussed in chapter 8, communal society has as its premise the end to private ownership of the means of production and the establishment of social ownership of the means of production. Presupposed is that those socially owned means of production are directed by the associated producers for the purpose of satisfying social needs. "Working with the means of production held in common," the producers are moved not by self-interest but by "communal needs and communal purposes."[2] In the organic system of community, the three sides of "the elementary triangle of socialism" are both premises and results of the system.

However, though social ownership of the means of production and social production organized by workers for the satisfaction of social needs are necessary, they are not sufficient for the reproduction of communal society. In particular, central to and permeating all aspects of this system is solidarity (communality) among the producers, and the system must reproduce this premise. If, for some reason, an emphasis upon "social preferences" is crowded out by material self-interest, communal society will not be a system of reproduction. Accordingly, to produce *homo solidaricus,* the system requires institutions and practices that reproduce solidarity, that provide negative feedback to any disturbances and thereby ensure homeostasis of the system.

These are not the only premises that must be reproduced. Marx explicitly indicated that the system must be sustainable. Just as he envisioned the all-round development of the producers in the system of community, so also did Marx stress that "the earth continuously improves, so long as it is treated correctly."[3] That requires understanding the "metabolism prescribed by the natural laws of life itself" and recognition of the "regulative law" of "systematic restoration" as the "inalienable condition for the existence and reproduction of the chain of human generations."[4] Essential for community as an organic system, in short, is that we grasp "the whole gamut of permanent conditions of life required by the chain of human generations."[5]

For this there is a specific premise. Viewing history backwards, Marx explained that "from the standpoint of a higher socio-economic formation," one premise of communal society would be the end to private ownership of portions of the earth:

Even an entire society, a nation, or all simultaneously existing societies taken together, are not the owners of the earth. They are simply its possessors, its beneficiaries, and have to bequeath it in an improved state to succeeding generations, as *boni patres familias*.[6]

The necessary premise for the "conscious and rational treatment of the land" that permits "the existence and reproduction of the chain of human generations" is that the land is "permanent communal property."[7]

As is the case for all the premises of community, the reproduction of sustainability is not a given, not a static state that, once achieved, rests. Rather, there is constant movement, constant tendencies that threaten reproduction. The first question of Levins and Lewontin was "in the face of constantly displacing influences, how do things remain recognizably what they are?" Their general answer was that "things are the way they are because of the actions of opposing processes," that is, that there is stability and equilibrium insofar as potential disruption is countered by negative feedback that permits the reproduction of the system. In the case of the system of community, *homo solidaricus* must act to ensure that the premises of community are reproduced if the system is to remain what it is.

The Original Development of the Premises of Community

But what has to happen in the present for the future to become what it must? From the vantage point of community, we ask the second question of Levins and Lewontin, "How did things get the way they are?"[8] How were the premises of community constructed? For Levins and Lewontin, "Things are the way they are because they got that way, and not because they have to be that way, or always were that way, or because it's the only way to be."

As we have seen, the movement from capitalism to community is not inevitable. True, capitalism constantly generates crises, but these contain within themselves self-correcting tendencies, including the power of capital's ideological hegemony. Further, even where a combination of crises and increased opposition to the system creates conditions in which "the original system can no longer persist as it was [and] the system may go into wider and wider fluctuations and breakdown," nothing ensures that its parts will be reassembled in a system of community as opposed to something else (for example, fascism).[9] This, as we have noted, is one of the limits of attempting to write history forward. The system of community does not emerge "because it's the only way to be."

When we write history backwards from community, we begin by identifying the central premises whose history we must attempt to trace. And here we need to emphasize that it is not social ownership of the means of production, nor organization of production by the producers, nor production for social needs that are the essential premises. Rather, as indicated above, solidarity among fully developed producers is the social relation that characterizes community as an organic system, and it is the development of this relation that must guide us.

Many elements may be assembled that point away from capitalism. We have seen, for example, that when workers act in common to struggle directly against capital over wages and working conditions, they change and make themselves increasingly fit to build a new society. And, as the struggle over the Ten Hours Bill indicated, this transformative process is not limited to battles with individual capitalists. In that political agitation, Engels wrote, workers became acquainted with one another and came "to a knowledge of their social position and interests" and were no longer the same as they were before. Surely, the same might be said of current political struggles for rent control, free transit, minimum wages, climate action, and, indeed, struggles against divisions, racial profiling by police, patriarchy, and, in general, for dignity. All of these transform people and build solidarity.

All such struggles—against oppression in the workplace, inequality, and the inability to satisfy needs—could be put in the framework of a struggle against the elementary triangle of capitalism. But in this path of negation there is something important missing: a vision of the future society. In themselves, nothing in these struggles points clearly to the qualities of communal society. *Our first critical question* is: What is the path to community if saying "no" is insufficient?

In contrast, there definitely are activities that provide glimpses of a society based upon solidarity and respect for the needs of others. People develop new qualities and capacities when they act in common based upon social preferences. New practices and institutions such as co-operatives, free stores, community gardens, participatory budgeting, and local planning do contribute to the formation of *homo solidaricus*. But how are these prefigurative activities to be connected to the struggles of negation described above? This is *our second critical question*. Further, these solidaristic activities in themselves tend to be dwarfish, much like Marx described the co-operatives of his time. Is the answer quantitative, that is, to accumulate (in size and extent) experiences of communal relations until a tipping point is reached?

The Path to Community Is No Royal Road

If the path to community involved the accumulation of one act of communal relations after another until they reached a critical mass, that path would be long but relatively smooth. However, as Preobrazhensky insisted about all new systems, the system of community does not develop "on the basis merely of the immanent laws which are inherent to the particular formation." It develops within contested reproduction. Rather than the unfolding of a germ increasingly realized, those glimpses of a future society are perceived by the working class that capital actively produces, a working class that is alienated, separated, self-interested, consumerist, and that looks upon the requirements of capital as "self-evident natural laws."

Workers produced concretely by capital are not a Platonic Idea but a historical product, the effect of capital's specific initiatives to divide the working class, initiatives both unique to its mode of production and those reflecting its ability to take advantage of all differences within the working class. Of course, those workers, as we have seen, are not only the product of capital. Once engaged in struggle, workers transform circumstances and themselves. And they do so through *all* their struggles because they are not defined solely by their direct relation to capital but are the ensemble of all their social relations.[10]

Yet the changes in people as the result of their various struggles do not automatically make them fit for communality. In the process of contested reproduction, there is interaction and interpenetration. Accordingly, the path to community cannot be "pure" but inevitably is "in every respect, economically, morally, and intellectually" infected by the old society, a whole in which the side of capital deforms the side of community. What is the result of that infection?

Every collective struggle of people for their common needs, however it may transform them, occurs in the context of the atomism and separation characteristic of capitalism. Because those engaged in struggle have a dual nature, both as people transforming themselves through their practice and as hosts of the second product of capital, their separation does not miraculously disappear. Accordingly, instead of a leap from individual atomism to community, the immediate result of their activity may be the development of *collective* atomism, a process in which differences within are reduced while differences outside the group are increased. As noted earlier, Engels pointed out that separation in different units "restricts the workers to seeing their interest in that of their employers, thus making every single section of workers into an auxiliary army for the class employing them."[11]

This tendency to view competitors as the Other was present in the market-self-managed enterprises of Yugoslavia. Solidarity among members of the collective was present because of their common interest in maximizing income per worker; however, there was solidarity neither with the workers of other enterprises, with which they competed or bargained, nor with the members of society as a whole. Loyalty to their own particular enterprise was demonstrated when 70 percent of self-managing agreements between enterprises (developed because the Yugoslav state was attempting to replace the anarchy of market forces with a medium-term process of planning from below) were abandoned unilaterally when inflation altered relative prices.

Thus, even in the case of workers' councils, essential for creating the space in which workers can develop their capacities through their activity, there is no automatic process by which those cells of a new socialist state will be linked. Rather, while they can build a unity of purpose within a worker-managed unit, they are isolated and self-oriented cells, and that collective atomism can make them indifferent, as in Yugoslavia, to the existence of inequality in society. In short, there is no spontaneous tendency for workers to identify their individual interests with those of the working class as a whole.[12]

There is a parallel here to the communal councils described by Chávez as cells of the new state. Here, too, solidarity develops among those who have learned to act in common; however, that solidarity does not necessarily extend beyond the geographical bounds of the community in question nor to individuals who are not viewed as members of the community. Establishing the boundaries of the community is seen as ensuring that the common property or commons that are the result of collective activity is not open-access property and thus subject to exhaustion by outsiders. Again, we see neither a stress upon ending inequality among communities nor an automatic process by which separate communities are linked.

There is, in short, a paradox of protagonism—a spontaneous tendency for increased solidarity within the given group to be accompanied by increased separation from those outside. How, then, can struggles be linked if the spontaneous tendency is toward collective atomism? When workers struggle against various aspects of their oppression, they develop capacities and solidarity among those in struggle, but they do not spontaneously generate links between their struggles. For example, what connects collective struggles over rent, climate justice, racism, healthcare, or police oppression? What counters the tendency for collective atomism, a tendency to insist upon walls between struggles? This is *a third critical question*. In the absence of a connection between struggles, these are separate islands in a capitalist sea, a sea characterized by the tendency to view the general requirements of capitalism (apart from the particular objects of struggle) as "self-evident natural laws."

Déjà Vu *All Over Again?*

Separation is not only horizontal. Capital produces and reproduces vertical separation, that between mental and manual labor, between those who think and those who do. It produces those who think they know and those who think they do not know. And this separation of the products of capital does not automatically disappear when workers begin to struggle against capital, because those workers are themselves "in every respect, economically, morally, and intellectually" infected by capital.

If you don't know where you've been, you may end up there again. It therefore would be a mistake to ignore the extent to which previous efforts to move along the path to community have reproduced characteristics inherited from capital. Consider, for example, the trade unions that Marx and Engels viewed as critical for achieving the immediate goals of workers.[13] That these organs created by the working class have proved inadequate for developing the capacities of workers early was stated succinctly by Rosa Luxemburg in her description of the internal structure of trade unions, where "the initiative and the power of making decisions thereby devolve upon trade union specialists, so to speak, and the more passive virtue of discipline upon the mass of members." Trade union preoccupation, then and now, with the goal of achieving that fair wage for a fair day's work that capital would deny has prevented the development of a second product that would challenge the rule of capital.[14]

A similar pattern may be seen in cooperatives and worker-managed enterprises. Although Marx praised the development of the cooperative movement as a great victory of the political economy of the working class ("social production controlled by social foresight"), he understood that these "first examples of the emergence of a new form" emerged "within the old form" and were reproducing "all the defects of the existing system." While he was concerned in particular by the way in which the cooperatives were based upon self-interest—indeed, "individual and antagonistic interests"—Marx did not explore the way in which their focus upon self-interest tended to foster hierarchical patterns once they went beyond "dwarfish forms."[15]

We can see that pattern clearly, however, in the experience of self-managed enterprises in Yugoslavia. Although juridically these firms were socially owned and under the control of workers' councils, the focus upon self-interest (maximizing income per worker) led workers to accept the recommendations of the managers, "the experts," as to how best to achieve these goals. As one Yugoslav writer commented twenty-five years after the law on workers' management, the worker had "only meagre opportunity for developing, in performing his duties, any substantial measure of freedom of thought, imagination and inventiveness."[16] In Mondragon as well, a pattern of activated managers and "passivity among workers" apparently has characterized the cooperative experience. "Far from generating *ekintza* [taking action]," argues Sharryn Kasmir in her study of Mondragon, the large multinational corporation and federation of worker cooperatives, which originated in the Basque Country in Spain, "cooperativism appears to engender apathy."[17] In such cases, the capacity-producing potential inherent in cooperative production was clearly not realized.

Add to this the tendency in parliamentary parties of the working class for the development of a gap between rank-and-file members and their parliamentary representatives and organizational functionaries. Based in particular upon his study of the German Social Democratic Party, sociologist Robert Michels in 1911 attributed the emergence of an oligarchy, indeed a "hierarchical bureaucracy," to the need and effect of organization. The impossibility of direct democracy with the growth of an organization and therefore the necessity of the mass to delegate responsibility to responsible and dedicated leaders, Michels argued, inevitably produces a professional leadership and the disempowering of the masses. Originating in technical requirements but reinforced by the transformation (in terms of life experience and psychology) of both leaders and the led, he insisted upon the operation of an "iron law of oligarchy" even in socialist parties dedicated to internal democracy.[18] That tendency, it must be admitted, has been reproduced repeatedly in parliamentary socialist parties.

As we saw in chapter 10, that which is unintentional, or at least unarticulated, in the above cases is for the vanguard party model the explicit principle of organization. Given its conviction that system change requires a disciplined, centralized, and united revolutionary vanguard to organize, guide, and orient the working class, the vanguard party opposes spontaneity and initiative both from below and outside its bounds.[19] Since the vanguard party, and it alone, knows how to build socialism, its perspective is characteristic of "the banking concept of education" described by Paulo Freire: "(a) the teacher teaches and the students are taught; (b) the teacher knows everything and the students know nothing; (c) the teacher thinks and the students are thought about." Substitute party for "teacher" and working class for "student," and you have a picture of the one-way street implicit in the vanguard party as it has existed in practice.[20]

In "real socialism," when the expression of the vanguard relation is armed with state power, the results have been predictable. The working class there is prevented from making decisions in the workplace and communities and is expected to follow directives from above. In return for accepting this subordinate position, the working class receives definite benefits such as secure employment, stable prices, subsidized necessities, and relative egalitarianism in a type of social contract. And, the result? As Freire commented, "The more completely they [students] accept the passive role imposed on them, the more they tend simply to adapt to the world as it is and to the fragmented view of reality deposited in them." The nature of the second product of "real socialism" was demonstrated by the passive acceptance by the working class of the restoration of capitalism.[21]

Is hierarchy as such the problem? If so, it would follow that any departure from pure horizontalism (including the election of representatives) must be avoided. That, however, would confuse the form of the problem for its content. The problem is not representation as such but rather the absence of revolutionary practice, the absence of the protagonism that builds capacities. And that brings us to *our fourth critical question*: given the tendency for the reproduction of hierarchy, how is it possible to proceed along the path to community?

Thus the four critical questions are: how to link struggles of negation to community, how to link prefigurative activities to struggles
of negation, how to link separate struggles, and how to fight the tendency for hierarchy. They all pose the same problem: in contested
reproduction between capitalism and community, there is no spontaneous path to community. To advance along that path, a political
instrument is essential.

12

The Political Instrument We Need

Two Streams from Hegel/Marx

The first stream we have followed from Hegel/Marx stresses the importance of understanding the whole. The truth is the whole, we learned from Hegel. And as Levins and Lewontin emphasize, the parts of a whole are not autonomous and independent but interpenetrate within the whole. On the other hand, changes in parts and new parts alter the whole and accordingly affect other parts within the whole. Thus, wholes make parts and parts make wholes.

We see that Marx employed the concept of an organic system, a whole in which all elements are both premises and results. This is how he presented capitalism as a system of reproduction in *Capital*. However, actually existing capitalism is not an organic system but contains elements not compatible with capitalism as an organic system. Marx understood that wholes are not necessarily organic systems. We see this, for example, in his description of so-called primitive accumulation of capital, which is a process of developing capitalism based not upon premises it produces but rather upon historic premises. This is quite distinct from capitalism once it has developed on its own foundations. Similarly, in his *Critique of the Gotha Programme,* we see the same distinction between communism as an organic system and that system as it emerges, where it is based upon premises that it has not itself developed (its "defects").

To explore a whole that is not characterized by an organic system, we introduced the concept of contested reproduction, where wholes contain elements of different organic systems that struggle to subordinate each other. This, as Marx noted, is how an organic system develops by successfully subordinating all elements of society to itself. In preceding chapters, we explored actually existing capitalism as a whole marked by contested reproduction between capitalism and community. Accordingly, the essential question for all revolutionaries is how can we succeed in making the system of community subordinate the capitalist system.

A second stream flowing from Hegel/Marx stresses self-development through activity. We saw very clearly Marx's embrace of Hegel's "outstanding achievement" in his conception of "the self-creation of man as a process," that is, of labor/activity "as man's act of self-genesis." That stream yields Marx's concept of revolutionary practice the simultaneous changing of circumstances and human activity or self-change. This is the basis for the recognition of a second product, the human product of activity, and thus the importance of protagonism in the development of human capacity.

Here was a consistent thread for Marx. We see his repeated argument that, by struggling in common, the working class makes itself fit to build a new society. Rather than as more or less well-fed instruments of production, the working class transforms "circumstances and men" through its struggles. Considered by itself, it goes beyond barriers to its development and posits a new society, a society of associated producers, a relation among producers that is characterized by community.

And yet, following Preobrazhensky, we know that the protagonism of the producers cannot be considered by itself because it occurs not in abstraction but in a whole marked by contested reproduction between capitalism and community. The two streams we have been reviewing, when joined, bring us to a significant result both theoretically and politically. Since parts are always shaped by their relations within the whole and are the product of interpenetration, in this contested reproduction the working class does not stand outside capital but is contained within it.

What are the implications of understanding the working class within this whole as the product of the interpenetration of capital? As we saw in the preceding chapter, the struggle of the working class against capital and for community is also a struggle *within* the working class against capital—a struggle versus atomism and separation, a struggle for solidarity and equality, a struggle against hierarchy and domination.

Against Spontaneity

To believe that the battle against capitalism and for community will succeed without a conscious struggle against inherent tendencies produced by capitalism is a comforting fairy tale. The hegemony of capital is not an accident nor is it the result of an inherited culture. Rather, the tendency within the working class to accept the rules of life under capitalism is reproduced spontaneously every day. Accordingly, to build the society of community we are left with the challenges with which we ended the last chapter: the need to link struggles of negation to community, to link prefigurative activities to struggles of negation, to link separate struggles, and to fight the tendency for hierarchy. Once we understand the interpenetration characteristic of contested reproduction, the necessity for the political instrument to combat spontaneity is obvious.

That has always been the tenet of the vanguard party. But you do not need to be a self-described Marxist-Leninist to insist upon the need for a political instrument to struggle to replace capitalism with community.[1] Decrying "the myth of the purely spontaneous revolution," Murray Bookchin, a self-described ex-anarchist, insisted that a revolutionary Left "must resolutely confront the problem of organization." Can we conceive, he asks, of "a popular movement gaining power without an agency that can provide it with guidance?" On the contrary, what is required is the "creation and maintenance of

an organization that is enduring, structured, and broadly program-
matic." Further, Bookchin stressed that this revolutionary agency
"must contain a responsible membership that firmly and knowledge-
ably adheres to its ideals; and it must advance a sweeping program for
social change that can be translated into everyday practice."[2]

Similarly, Marta Harnecker consistently argued that overcoming
the hegemony of capital and constructing a new popular hegemony
"will not occur spontaneously; we need a political instrument, a political organization to help us to construct it."[3] To change the correlation
of forces, it is essential to construct the social and political forces that
will "make possible in the future what today appears impossible.
. . . But this construction of forces cannot occur spontaneously. It
requires a political instrument that is capable of consciously building
the required forces."[4]

In particular, the political instrument we need is one that
recognizes, as did Marx, that "where the worker is regulated bureaucratically from childhood onwards, where he believes in authority, in
those set over him, the main thing is *to teach him to walk by himself*."[5]
It is one that stresses the critical necessity to build the capacities of the
working class. That means a focus upon the human product of revolutionary practice. Accordingly, in *A World to Build*, Harnecker argued
that this was the most important task of the political instrument:

> Finally, we have the most important task, because without it
> we will never be able to build socialism. What is needed is a
> political instrument that encourages popular protagonism in
> the most varied social and political milieus in the country,
> one that puts itself at the service of that participation so that it
> is the people themselves who build the new society. . . . Only
> thus will we be true to the thesis that revolutionary practice
> is essential for workers' emancipation and that of the popular
> movement in general. It is through practice that full human
> development is reached, this being the most important goal we
> are aiming for.[6]

Revolutionary Practice

Recall the dialectical relation of acts and capacities in which acts create capacities, capacities enable acts. Capacity, Lucien Sève indicated, is "the ensemble of actual potentialities, innate or acquired, to carry out any act whatever and whatever its level."[7] Accordingly, by stressing a "political instrument that encourages popular protagonism in the most varied social and political milieus in the country," Harnecker communicates that, by struggling with respect to *all* aspects of its social relations, the working class develops the capacities that will permit it to defeat capital.

We have already seen how direct struggles against the capital relation help the working class to transform itself. But revolutionary practice is not limited to this sphere nor is the role of the political instrument. The struggles against racism and patriarchy, for example, transform people so they can enter into all their relations with this new potentiality. They change circumstances—for example, through victories in battles—and simultaneously invest in the development of their capacities.

Once we start from the centrality of revolutionary practice, we understand that organizational forms matter. The large mass meeting inspires and communicates a sense of strength. In itself, however, it does not build capacity. Rather, as Harnecker argued, you need spaces small enough both to facilitate "the protagonism of those attending by making them feel comfortable and encouraging them to speak freely" and also to allow them to engage in the multiplicity of acts that can build their capacities.[8] You need, in short, to create spaces that allow people to take those steps through which they transform themselves.

Yet small spaces for protagonism are not the goal; nor is it a confederation of freely associated communities that for anarchists is the alternative to a "state." Rather, when you "decentralize all that you can decentralize," the principle that Harnecker identifies as "subsidiarity," the central point is to build the capacities of people.[9] As Harnecker and economist José Bartolomé say in *Planning from Below*, decentralized participatory planning contributes to "the process of building the capacities of the citizens through their own concrete experiences and practice." and "those who involve themselves are transformed; they are no longer the same persons they were at the start of the process."[10]

In everyday life, there are many opportunities to create the spaces in which the protagonism of people is fostered. Consider in this context the municipality or city as an important site in which people can act in common. Struggles for tenant rights, free public transit, support for public and co-op housing, increasing citywide minimum wages, initiating community gardens, climate action at the neighborhood and community level, immigrant support, and opposition to racial profiling and police oppression—all have the potential for people to develop their capacities and a sense of strength.

Further, the municipality is a space where electoral activity based upon a combination of such struggles can support the development of new spaces for protagonism. Such a combination of the state and protagonism is proposed at the local level by Bookchin, who makes "libertarian municipalism" the core of his perspective and explicitly argues that elected officials at the municipal level should use their power "to legislate popular assemblies into existence."[11]

Small spaces, however, do not mean small struggles. Rather, they are the form that allows for the combination of nationwide struggles with the process of building capacities. Thus struggles to end capitalist ownership of particular sectors or to end the destruction of the environment, for example, are strengthened by being rooted in local organization that simultaneously builds a basis for further advances. To stress this point is to recognize the necessity to walk on two legs, in order to (a) take the old state away from capital; and (b) to build a new state through institutions such as workers' and communal councils that develop the capacities of the working class. As I argued in *The Socialist Imperative*, for successful struggle to build the new society through a combination of the nurturing of the new state and the withering away of the old, the party that is needed is one that learns to walk on two legs.[12]

Traditional Models

Unfortunately, the classic political instruments we know have not emphasized the centrality of protagonism because they have focused upon one leg, the necessity to capture the existing state from capital. Some have approached this by stressing particular inadequacies of capitalist governments such as government austerity measures. In this tradition, socialist Vivek Chibber argued in 2017 that popular movements at the time demonstrated that "what is in crisis right now is the neoliberal *model* of capitalism, not *capitalism* itself." Indeed, Chibber stressed that the Left must accept that any belief in the possibility of a revolutionary rupture with capitalism at this time is "entirely hallucinatory." Why? Because, in contrast with the past, the state has "infinitely greater legitimacy with the population." That is, we must acknowledge "the political stability of the state" and therefore must forget about the "centrality of a revolutionary rupture and navigate a more gradualist approach."[13]

While Chibber's more gradualist approach has two wings: (1) a "mass cadre-based party" rooted in the working class; and (2) an electoral strategy that builds upon mobilization at the base to make inroads in the state in order to weaken capital and strengthen the working class, he admits that the first simply does not exist. Rather, "at this moment, the parliamentary dimension seems to be opening up faster than the one at the base." Accordingly, Chibber is one of many who seized upon the importance of the electoral path through the Democratic Party: "The Left should jump in, capitalize on it, and then use its gains to build the base."[14] Every crisis, he notes, finds a resolution, and the current crisis of the neoliberal model provides an opportunity "if we play our cards right." Given that perspective, his conclusion follows: "We must start down the road of social democracy and then to democratic socialism."

That road to social democracy starts with support for "good" capitalism versus "bad" capitalism. Whether it identifies the conjuncture as one marked by a crisis of neoliberalism or whether it submerges a critique of capitalism as such for electoral purposes, its organizational vehicle is the same, an electoral party that attempts to take advantage of popular discontent with neoliberalism. [15] While it is possible that a combination of contingent factors under these circumstances might allow a Left (or Left coalition) to win an election and become a governing power, I argued in *Build It Now* that any government that seriously would challenge neoliberalism would immediately face the assorted weapons of capital such as capital strikes; accordingly, the choice before it would be to give in or move in. For the latter, it would have to break ideologically and politically with capital. If it failed to do so, "the policies of such a government inevitably will disappoint and demobilize all those looking for an alternative to neoliberalism; and, once again, its immediate product will be the conclusion that there is no alternative."[16]

That, unfortunately, is the familiar story of social democracy as a political instrument. "Starting down the road of social democracy" can produce a path dependency that leads to support of capitalism at best and, at worst, the stimulation of fascist alternatives. The relatively recent case of Syriza, the coalition of the radical Left in Greece, offers a dramatic negative example. [17] Growing because of its support for the struggles of people in the streets, Syriza declared at its founding congress as a unitary party in July 2013 that its goal was socialism for the twenty-first century. It would break with capital, on the one hand, by cancelling the policy memoranda between international finance capital and the Greek neoliberal government and, among other things, would place the banking system under public ownership and audit the national debt to cancel its onerous terms.

On the other hand, having learned from the struggles in the streets of the social and political movements, a Syriza government would introduce the concept and practice of democratic planning and social control at all levels of central and local government and would promote democracy in the workplace through workers' councils composed of representatives elected by and recallable by workers. Syriza's explicit goal, in short, was not social democracy. Syriza understood that building socialism for the twenty-first century requires you to walk on two legs, both to capture the existing state in order to reverse policies supportive of capital and also to build and nurture the elements of a new socialist state based upon self-government from below.[18]

But the desire for electoral success based upon the existing correlation of forces proved too strong. Syriza's electoral program presented in September 2014 contained no pledge to cancel the memoranda, no call for public ownership of the banks, and, in place of any anti-capitalist (let alone socialist) measures, proposed a National Reconstruction Plan, a Keynesian program of public investment and tax reduction for the middle class. Further, there was little sign of the earlier determination to use the state to foster development of the cells of a new state, nothing that challenged capital as the demand for workers' councils and workers' control would have. Everything in the electoral program was consistent with support for capital. The proposal contained in that program was to walk on two legs along the road to social democracy.

As so often, going down the road to social democracy led not to democratic socialism but to the reinforcement of capitalism. Following its successful election, Syriza proceeded from initial retreats in post-electoral negotiations with finance capital to successive surrenders to ultimate rout and capitulation. Every illusion in social democracy should have been dispelled by the Syriza government's refusal to accept the verdict of the population when it rejected the popular referendum in July 2015 against austerity proposals.

The debacle of Syriza did not come as a surprise in Greece to those who were always suspicious of its social democracy. But not only them. For those who view the crisis as not one of neoliberalism but rather as that of the capitalist economy as such, the accommodations of social democracy everywhere ultimately support capitalism. In this alternative view of the conjuncture, capitalism has entered (or is on the threshold of) an economic crisis that will demonstrate to all that the economic system is no longer viable and must be replaced. Rather than periodic crises of overaccumulation and of the underproduction of surplus value (both considered in chapter 4), capitalism now faces the "Big One," the apocalypse promised according to this reading of *Capital*.

Accordingly, from this perspective, the political instrument required is a disciplined and centralized organization that can lead the working class through the ensuing chaos produced by the coming crisis. That is the logic underlying the classical vanguard party discussed in chapter 10. As I argued in *The Contradictions of "Real Socialism*, given its understanding of the need for a political instrument to defeat the enemies of the working class in order to replace capitalism with socialism, this perspective insists upon "a disciplined, centralized and united revolutionary party—our party."[19] To prepare the vanguard party is thus the principal task of organization.

Two problems with this perspective, however, were identified in earlier chapters. One, discussed in chapter 4, is that its certainty about the existing or pending ultimate crisis forgets that capital is not passive and continually searches for means to go beyond all barriers to its growth, barriers manifested in falling profit rates. Those who emphasize the coming capitalist crisis forget the negative feedback in the system that reverses extended crises. Indeed, alternating phases of boom tend to be seen as mere aberrations, epiphenomena that pave the way for ever-greater future collapses. Theory rules, impervious to all developments that may challenge it.

The second problem, as we have stressed, is the working class this theory presumes. Rather than recognizing that capitalism tends to produce a working class that looks upon capital's requirements as "self-evident natural laws," the militance of their idealized working class needs merely a kiss at the appropriate time to awaken to its appointed tasks. However, in the absence of a working class that has developed its capacities through its protagonism, the existing working class is the product of capital. What Lukàcs called the immaturity of the working class ensures that capitalist crises will be resolved through capital's initiatives. Unfortunately, rather than addressing this problem, those with this perspective often look upon social movements as fertile ground for the recruitment of cadres for the disciplined phalanxes with which they can celebrate the distilled purity of their brands and their preparedness for the next October.

Obviously, there are major differences between those who reject a revolutionary rupture and stress electoral gains versus those dedicated to building the vanguard party. However, neither identifies the capacity of the working class as the central problem. For one, the working class as it exists needs an electoral program consistent with its consciousness (and of a coalition with other sectors of society). For the other, the working class as it exists will be transformed by a crisis external to it that makes it the working class that it must be and thus receptive to the revolutionary program. Missing in both is a focus upon building the working class as a process. However, in the absence of a working class that has developed its capacity, dignity, and strength through its protagonism and practice, the immediate response of workers to crises is to accept the necessity for the reproduction of capitalism.

The Political Instrument as Revolutionary Pedagogue

As we have seen, encouraging the development of the capacities of the working class is the most important task of the political instrument. But how is this to be done? Drawing upon her observation and analysis of the practice of Latin American parties, Harnecker identified serious problems with respect to their relations with social and political movements as well as their internal governance. Those problems, it will be recognized, are not unique to Latin America.

In proposition after proposition in "Ideas for the Struggle," Harnecker stresses the need to correct bad practices. She points, for example, to the tendencies of political instruments with respect to social movements to instruct, manipulate, impose leadership from above, and, in general, to disrespect their autonomy. Indeed, her criticisms are crystallized in the titles of two of her propositions: "Convince, not impose" and "Be at the service of popular movements, not replace them."[20]

These undesirable practices correspond to what Paulo Freire called the "banking concept" of education where the teacher (leader) deposits knowledge into the minds of the students whose role is to receive, memorize, and repeat that knowledge. A conception of education in which it is presumed that the students are ignorant and remain passive, this is education that supports oppression because it encourages students to adapt to the world as it is.[21] But that conception is not limited to those who consciously or unconsciously support the oppressor; it is retained by many who "truly desire to transform the unjust order" but "believe that they must be the executors of the transformation. They talk about the people, but they do not trust them."[22]

In contrast to this approach, marked by manipulation, propaganda, sloganizing, communiqués from above and outside, Freire offers the concept of "problem-posing education" in which there is dialogue between teacher and student such that the student teaches and the teacher learns. Rather than treating people "as objects which must be saved from a burning building," he insists that "the correct method for a revolutionary leadership ... lies in dialogue. The conviction of the oppressed that they must fight for their liberation is not a gift bestowed by the revolutionary leadership, but the result of their own *conscientizacao* [critical consciousness]."[23] Rather than treating people as depositories of someone else's knowledge, revolutionary leadership puts trust in people that through their own practice they can develop their capacity (and they do). At its core, Freire's revolutionary pedagogy is based upon Marx's concept of revolutionary practice.

Rather than the vertical relation characteristic of the banking concept of education, the revolutionary political instrument requires a horizontal relationship between the political instrument and social movements. That political instrument is a space, Harnecker argued,

> that respects the autonomy of the social movements instead of manipulating them. And whose militants and leaders are true popular pedagogues capable of stimulating the knowledge that exists within the people . . . and through the fusion of this knowledge with the most all-encompassing knowledge that the political organization can offer.[24]

The relation between the political instrument and social movements, Harnecker stressed, must be "a two-way circuit: from the political organization to the social movement and vice versa. Unfortunately, the tendency continues to be that it only functions in the first direction." In this respect, "it is important to learn to listen and to engage in dialogue with the people." Political instruments are not the only ones "capable of generating creative, new, revolutionary and transformative ideas." Accordingly, their role is "not only to echo the demands of the social movements, but also to gather ideas and concepts from these movements to enrich their own conceptual arsenal."[25]

It should be clear, she insisted, that "the type of political cadres we need cannot be cadres with a military mentality." On the contrary, "Political cadres should fundamentally be popular pedagogues, capable of fostering the ideas and initiatives that emerge from within the grassroots movement." When it is not preestablished schemes but "their own ideas and initiatives [that] are being put into action, they will see themselves as the protagonists of change and their capacity to struggle will enormously increase."[26]

What the political instrument brings to this dialogue is an understanding of the necessity for linking separate struggles and of the need to fight against the attempt of the enemy to divide and weaken the working class. Further, the all-encompassing knowledge that the political instrument as popular pedagogue has to offer the social movements is its grasp of the relation between the elements of community (such as acting in common and social preferences) and their current struggles. In this respect, the political instrument represents in the movement of the present "the future of that movement."[27]

Both with respect to the relation between the political instrument and social movements and also within the political movement itself, Harnecker's "Ideas for the Struggle" insists upon the need to "eliminate all verticalism that stifles the initiative of the people." Thus, within the political instrument, she insists upon the necessity of real democratization and tolerance. "Minorities can be right" is the topic of one "Idea," where she argues that minorities should be respected and that they have a duty to continue fighting to defend their ideas precisely because they may be right. Further, it is necessary to respect differences and to avoid attempting to homogenize militants according to a single norm. In this respect, she proposes that we must avoid rigidity and "create a type of organization that can house the widest range of militants, allowing for diverse levels of membership."[28]

We need to say more about the internal characteristics of the political instrument that can foster the ideas of people in social movements. How, for example, do you foster the development of political cadres as popular pedagogues rather than as those having a military mentality? The relation of cadres to movements cannot be separated from the way they are formed internally. Verticalism, however, is built into a structure in which discipline and acceptance of the decisions of higher bodies are characteristics of daily life in between policy conventions. As discussed in the section "Finally, the Party" in *The Socialist Alternative*:

> Further, understanding the way in which hierarchical structures can sap the creative energy and enthusiasm of those committed to the struggle to put an end to capital points to the need to make the base of any party structure the space for initiatives. Rather than the insistence upon uniform forms of participation (in the workplace or community), the possibility of autonomous collectives and affinity groups organized according to their interests. Rather than information and instructions passing vertically, the sharing and emulation of ideas and experiences horizontally. Rather than a single line of march in this asymmetrical warfare against capital, guerrilla units functioning under a general line and understanding the need for unity in struggle for major battles—how else to unleash creative energy and foster the revolutionary practice that can produce the people who can defeat capital?[29]

If political cadres are to come to social movements not with "banked knowledge" but with a deep understanding of the centrality of protagonism, it is because they themselves are its product and are reproduced daily as such by their practice within the political instrument itself.

The Crisis of the Earth System Revisited

But do we have the time for revolutionary pedagogy? The gradualness implicit in the focus upon the development of capacities appears in stark contrast to the immediacy that the crisis of the Earth System demands. Storms, drought, floods, pollution, disease, disappearing species, pandemics—all manifest this crisis that now threatens the original source of all wealth (human beings and nature) with extinction. Things, we are coming to understand, cannot go on as they have.

In contrast to crises of capital as such, the crisis of the Earth System does not contain within itself negative feedback that can mitigate the crisis. Rather, this crisis is qualitatively different. The crisis of the Earth System demonstrates that there was always something outside the social sphere, something outside of but necessary for it, namely, the natural sphere. Very simply, the whole that we have thought of as the combination of elements of capitalism and community never was the true whole. Rather, the whole is the Earth System, which contains both the social sphere and the natural sphere. In focusing only upon the former, we consider the Earth System one-sidedly.

Of course, the signs of something more were always there. Marx posed the possibility of lagging productivity in agriculture and extractive industries because "the productivity of labour is also bound up with natural conditions, which are often less favourable as productivity rises—as far as that depends on social conditions." Similarly, he identified the significance of "animal organic processes" and "vegetable organic processes," cases where "certain organic laws" were operative. Marx was pointing here to the separate metabolic process by which nature converts various inputs and transforms them into the basis for its reproduction. What are the implications of treating the existence of this natural side only through a collection of concrete observations?

If we fail to incorporate the side of nature explicitly, we are considering the Earth System one-sidedly and as an afterthought theoretically. Recall that Levins and Lewontin pointed out that Hegel's declaration that "the truth is the whole" is an aspiration and a guide: "We always have to be aware that there is more out there that might overwhelm our theories and thwart our best intentions." Indeed, failing to incorporate new sides of categories under investigation and "seizing upon one side of a dichotomous pair or a contradiction as if it were the whole thing," can infect our concept of the whole with "one-sidedness." Accordingly, they noted that "it is always necessary to recognize . . . that an 'object' kicks and screams when it is abstracted from its context and may take its revenge in leading us astray."[30]

The crisis of the Earth System today is the product of the particular interaction between a social sphere dominated by capital and the natural sphere. That interaction and interpenetration of parts produces a particular whole, one in which each side is shaped by that interaction. With different parts, there is a different Earth System. Consider a whole in which there is interaction between the sphere of nature and a social sphere dominated instead by community. In this case, society focuses upon understanding nature's own metabolism and recognizing "systematic restoration" as "the inalienable condition for the existence and reproduction of the chain of human generations." What community draws upon from nature, it attempts to restore. Characteristic of this "inverse situation" based upon the needs of human beings is a social metabolism in which "the earth continuously improves, so long as it is treated correctly," an Earth System marked by harmony between society and nature.

The social metabolism of capitalism, in contrast, is propelled by the drive for surplus value, a drive that produces the metabolic rift between society and nature characteristic of the existing Earth System. Always inherent in this particular whole has been the exhaustion and deformation of nature, an exhaustion that capital assumed could never happen but that now has come to characterize the current conjuncture with a vengeance. The imperative at this time, accordingly, is to put an end to capital and to attempt to repair the Earth

System; it is to move decisively to replace capitalism with community in the social sphere.

Contested Reproduction and the Rupture We Need

In the interregnum between capitalism and community, contested reproduction takes the form (as indicated in chapter 8) of material incentive versus social preferences, atomism versus community, separation versus solidarity, *homo economicus* versus *homo solidaricus*, and the political economy of capital versus the political economy of the working class. Into this mix, the crisis of the Earth System brings with it a struggle over who will bear the burden of this crisis. Capital, of course, has its usual weapons. It can attempt to intensify the separation of workers by encouraging racism and anti-immigrant mobilization, and it can use its state to enforce separation, austerity, and new forms of domination of the working class.

In their defense, workers organize to avoid bearing the burden of the crisis. However, to the extent that workers are the product of capital, even if they come to recognize the succession of discrete and often geographically separate events (floods, drought, disease, etc.) as indicators of a crisis of the Earth System, nothing inherently leads them to an understanding of that crisis as the result of capitalism as such rather than of short-sighted policies that can be corrected. In this respect, the solutions they tend to support are wholly consistent with the reproduction of capitalism.

Nevertheless, as in the case of the struggle over the working day, the protagonism of people produces them differently. There is a further element that points beyond capitalism. Manifestations of the crisis of the Earth System spontaneously may foster elements of community such as "solidarity, cooperation, care, reciprocity, mutualism, altruism, compassion, and love" (as in the response to the current Covid-19 pandemic).[31] This potential, however, is not necessarily realized. Just as no temperature will turn a stone into a chicken, global warming in itself will not turn workers into the revolutionary subjects needed to prevent extinction. As stressed above, to link the various threads of an alternative to capitalism requires a political instrument.

The crisis of the Earth System corresponds to a system breakdown as described by Levins and Lewontin:

> The stability or persistence of a system depends on a particular balance of positive and negative feedbacks, on parameters governing the rates of processes falling within certain limits. But these parameters, although treated in mathematical models as constants, are real-world objects that are themselves subject to change. Eventually some of those parameters will cross the threshold beyond which the original system can no longer persist as it was. The equilibrium is broken. The system may go into wider and wider fluctuations and break down, or the parts themselves, which have meaning only within a particular whole, may lose their identity as parts and give rise to a qualitatively new system.[32]

The Earth System as it exists faces such a rupture. But what kind of rupture? One centered in the natural sphere or one centered in the social sphere? An end to capitalist domination of the social sphere would point beyond the destruction of the natural sphere. Although it is possible that the severity of the crisis at a given time may create conditions in which an anti-capitalist party is able to become the governing power, to avoid repeating the experience of social democracy, "it must not only use that opportunity to defeat the logic of capital and to reduce capital's power over the state but also to use the power it has to foster the accelerated development of the sprouts of the new state."[33]

While there may be days, as Marx commented, "into which 20 years are compressed," building the capacities of the working class and the constituent elements of the new state from below generally does not occur overnight.[34] That apparent gradualness, though, is not the antithesis of a revolutionary rupture. The crisis of the Earth System creates the opportunity for the political instrument to build spaces for protagonism; and the resulting development of capacities changes the correlation of forces within the whole and provides the basis for a revolutionary rupture. "When a system is poised on the brink of a qualitative change," Levins and Lewontin point out, small events may produce major effects. Accordingly, "The task of promoting change is one of promoting the conditions under which small, local events can precipitate the desired restructuring."[35]

What must we do in the present for the future to become what it must? Obviously, given the existing crisis of the Earth System, we must try to put an end to capitalism by all means possible and as soon as possible. Every manifestation of that crisis such as the current pandemic provides an opportunity to educate, organize, and build the capacities of the working class. Through the development of a political instrument focused upon the centrality of human capacity, we can promote the conditions for the revolutionary rupture in which the system of community can replace capitalism.

Notes

Preface

1. Marx noted that characteristic of these efforts to prove the theory correct was "crass empiricism," "phrases in a scholastic way," and "cunning argument." See the discussion of Marx's disciples in "Why Beyond *Capital*?," in chap. 2 of Michael A. Lebowitz, *Beyond* Capital: *Marx's Political Economy of the Working Class*, 2nd ed. (New York: Palgrave Macmillan, 2003), esp. 20–21.

2. Michael A. Lebowitz, "The One-Sidedness of Capital," *Review of Radical Political Economics* 14/ 4 (1982); Lebowitz, 2003.

3. More recently, the study of Marx's late notebooks on ecological matters has revealed another critical silence in *Capital* as handed down. See in particular Kohei Saito, *Karl Marx's Ecosocialism: Capital, Nature and the Unfinished Critique of Political Economy* (New York: Monthly Review Press, 2017).

4. Michael A. Lebowitz, *Build It Now: Socialism for the Twenty-First Century* (New York: Monthly Review Press, 2006); *The Socialist Alternative: Real Human Development* (New York: Monthly Review Press, 2010); *The Socialist Imperative: From Gotha to Now* (New York: Monthly Review Press, 2015).

5. See "A New Political Instrument for a New Hegemony," Part 3 in Marta Harnecker, *A World to Build: New Paths toward Twenty-First Century Socialism* (New York: Monthly Review Press, 2015).

Introduction

1. Michael A. Lebowitz, *Beyond* Capital: *Marx's Political Economy of the Working Class* (New York: Palgrave Macmillan, 2003).

2. E. P. Thompson, *The Poverty of Theory* (New York: Monthly Review Press, 1978), 65.

3. Ibid.,106-7.

4. Cornelius Castoriadis, "On the History of the Workers' Movement," *Telos* 30 (Winter 1976-77): 33, n33; "An Interview," *Telos* 23 (Spring 1975): 144-45; Thompson, *The Poverty of Theory*, 59-62. As will be seen in the chapters that follow, my consideration of wage-labor as premise and result of capitalism as an organic system has brought me much closer to Thompson's position.

5. Thompson, *The Poverty of Theory*, 163-64, 167, 61.

6. Karl Marx, *Capital*, vol. 1 (New York: Vintage Books, 1977), 718.

7. Lebowitz, *Beyond* Capital, 2003, 63.

8. Ibid., 65.

9. Robert Albritton, "Returning to Marx's *Capital*: A Critique of Lebowitz's *Beyond* Capital: *History of Economic Ideas* 11, 2009:95-107. All citations can be found in "Beyond the *Capital* of Uno-ism," chap. 17 in Michael A. Lebowitz, *Following Marx: Method, Critique, and Crisis* (Chicago: Haymarket Books, 2009).

10. Ben Fine, "Debating Lebowitz: Is Class Conflict the Moral and Historical Element in the Value of Labour-Power?," *Historical Materialism* 16 (2008): 107. On "the degree of separation of workers," see Lebowitz, *Beyond* Capital, 2003, "Wages," chap. 6, 115-17, 216.

11. Fine, "Debating Lebowitz," 110.

12. Ibid., 108.

13. Ibid.

14. See my extended response to Fine in Michael A. Lebowitz, "Trapped Inside the Box? Five Questions for Ben Fine," *Historical Materialism* 18/1 (March 2010).

15. Alex Callinicos, *Deciphering Capital: Marx's Capital and Its Destiny* (London: Bookmarks, 2014), 304, 309.

16. Marx, *Capital*, vol. 1, 344, 348, 381.

17. Ibid., 342, 344.

18. Ibid., 348, 390, 395, 405, 409, 412-13.

19. Callinicos, *Deciphering Capital*, 309-10.

1. The Atomism of Neoclassical Economics

1. This chapter draws upon a talk presented to IAEDEN (Instituto de Altos Estudios de la Defensa Nacional), the Institute for Higher Studies of the Venezuelan Military, May 25, 2010. in Caracas, Venezuela.

2. Thorstein Veblen, "Why Is Economics Not an Evolutionary Science?" in *Veblen on Marx, Race, Science and Economics* (New York: Capricorn, 1969), 73.

3. Armen Alchian, "Information Costs, Pricing and Resource Unemployment," *Western Economic Journal* (June 1969).
4. E. K. Hunt, *History of Economic Thought: A Critical Perspective* (Belmont, CA: Wadsworth, 1979), 288.
5. J. K. Galbraith, *American Capitalism* (Boston: Houghton Mifflin, 1952), 52.
6. Richard Lewontin and Richard Levins, *Biology Under the Influence: Dialectical Essays on Ecology, Agriculture and Health* (New York: Monthly Review Press, 2007), 65.
7. Nikolai Bukharin, *Economic Theory of the Leisure Class* (New York: Monthly Review Press, 1972), 41.
8. See my discussion in "Analytical Marxism and the Marxian Theory of Crisis," in Lebowitz, *Following Marx*.

2. The Truth Is the Whole

1. Richard Levins and Richard Lewontin, *The Dialectical Biologist* (Harvard University Press, 1985).
2. Richard Lewontin and Richard Levins, *Biology Under the Influence*, 131.
3. G. W. F. Hegel, *The Phenomenology of Mind* (New York: Harper Torchbooks, 1967), 81–82.
4. Karl Marx, *Grundrisse* (New York: Vintage Books, 1973), 156.
5. Georg Lukács, *History and Class Consciousness: Studies in Marxist Dialectics* (Cambridge, MA: MIT Press, 1972), 27.
6. Levins and Lewontin, *The Dialectical Biologist*, 3, 269, 273.
7. V. I. Lenin, *Collected Works,* vol. 38: *Philosophical Notebooks* (Moscow: Foreign Languages Publishing House, 1961), 97,146–47, 159.
8. Bertell Ollman, *Dance of the Dialectic: Steps in Marx's Method* (Chicago: University of Illinois Press, 2003), 14.
9. Lewontin and Levins, *Biology Under the Influence*, 109, 131.
10. Ibid., 109.
11. Lenin, *Philosophical Notebooks*, 196.
12. Levins and Lewontin, *The Dialectical Biologist*, 275.
13. Ollman, *Dance of the Dialectic*, 18.
14. Marx, *Grundrisse*, 100.
15. Lenin, *Philosophical Notebooks*, 159.
16. Engels to Schmidt, October 27, 1890, in Marx and Engels, *Collected Works,* vol. 49, 63.
17. Lenin, *Philosophical Notebooks*, 139–41.
18. Lewontin and Levins, *Biology Under the Influence*, 86, 94, 115.
19. Ibid., 94–95, 109, 116.
20. Ibid., 116.

21. Ibid., 69, 138, 157.
22. Levins and Lewontin, *The Dialectical Biologist*, 280.
23. Ibid., 282
24. Lewontin and Levins, *Biology Under the Influence*, 77, 182.
25. Ibid., 85, 108.
26. Marx, *Grundrisse*, 100–101.
27. Lenin, *Philosophical Notebooks*, 146.
28. Lebowitz, *Beyond* Capital; Lebowitz, *Following Marx.*
29. Marx, *Grundrisse,* 100–101.
30. Henri Lefebvre, *Dialectical Materialism* (London: Jonathan Cape, 1968), 31.
31. G. W. F. Hegel, *Hegel's Science of Logic*, vol. 1 (London: Allen & Unwin, 1929), 65.
32. Ibid., 2:482–83.
33. See Lebowitz, *Beyond* Capital, for a complete discussion.
34. Lenin, *Philosophical Notebooks*, 19.
35. Ollman, *Dance of the Dialectic*, 23.
36. Ibid., 60.
37. Lewontin and Levins, *Biology Under the Influence*, 150–51.
38. Ibid., 150.
39. Ibid., 108.
40. Ibid., 123.
41. Lukács, *History and Class Consciousness*, 1; Lebowitz, *Beyond* Capital, 16, 25–26.

3. Marx's Conceptualization of Capitalism as an Organic System

1. Karl Marx, *Grundrisse,* 278.
2. Karl Marx, *Capital*, vol. 3 (New York: Vintage Books, 957.
3. Karl Marx, *Capital*, vol. 2 (New York: Vintage Books, 180–81.
4. Marx, *Capital,* 1:711.
5. Marx, *Capital*, 1:723.
6. Marx, *Capital*, 1:72.
7. Marx, *Grundrisse,* 459–60.
8. Karl Marx, *Poverty of Philosophy*, in Marx and Engels, *Collected Works*, vol. 6, 166–67.
9. Lewontin and Levins, *Biology Under the Influence*, 95–96.
10. Marx, *Capital,* 1:873–75.
11. Marx, *Grundrisse,* 460–61.
12. Ibid., 459–460.
13. Questions related to actually existing capitalism when it is not an organic system are explored below in chapter 9, "Between Organic Systems."

14. Marx, *Capital*, 1:1033.
15. See Lebowitz, *Beyond* Capital, chapter 4 for a discussion of the two circuits, in particular, the error in not recognizing the necessary circuit of wage-labor.
16. Marx, *Grundrisse*, 171–72.
17. Marx, *Capital*, 1:270–74.
18. See consideration of social relations within the household, including exploration of patriarchy as a slave relation, in chapter 8, "The One-Sidedness of Wage-Labour," Lebowitz, *Beyond* Capital.
19. Marx, *Capital*, 1:718–9, 290; *Marx, Grundrisse*, 676; Lebowitz, *Beyond* Capital: 63–74.
20. Marx, *Capital*, 1:291–2.
21. Marx, *Capital*, 1:709.
22. Marx, *Capital*, 2:109.
23. Marx, *Capital*, 1:715–16.
24. Marx, *Capital*, 1:899, 904–5.
25. Marx, *Capital*, 1:548, 643, 799.
26. Marx, *Capital*, 1:482–84, 548, 607–8, 614.
27. Marx, *Grundrisse*, 488.
28. Ibid., 287; Lebowitz, *Beyond* Capital, 32–44.
29. Marx, *Grundrisse*, 694; Marx, *Capital*, 1: 1058. Further, the real existence of capital as many capitals in competition tends to produce the dependence of workers upon the particular capitals that employ them. Lebowitz, *Beyond* Capital, 157–58.
30. Marx, *Capital*, 1:899.
31. Marx, *Capital*, 1:899, 935.
32. Marx, *Capital*, 1:899.

4. Crises and Non-Reproduction

1. Karl Marx, *Theories of Surplus Value*, vol. 2 (Moscow: Progress Publishers, 1968), 394, 504–5, 509.
2. Ibid., 2:514.
3. Karl Marx, *Grundrisse*, 443. Emphasis added.
4. Marx, *Grundrisse*, 447. Marx made the same point in *Theories of Surplus Value*, vol. 3 (Moscow: Progress Publishers, 1971): "It is *crises* that put an end to this apparent *independence* of the various elements of which the production process continually consists and which it continually reproduces" (518).
5. Marx, *Theories of Surplus Value*, 2:165, 500.
6. Marx, *Grundrisse*, 443–44.
7. Marx, *Grundrisse*, 420.
8. Karl Marx, *Capital*, vol. 2, n391.

9. Karl Marx, *Capital*, vol. 3, 352, 365.

10. Marx, *Grundrisse*, 421.

11. Marx: *Grundrisse*, 415; Marx, *Theories of Surplus Value*, 2:528.

12. Marx, *Grundrisse*, 422.

13. Marx, *Theories of Surplus Value*, 2:468.

14. Marx, *Capital*, 2:497.

15. Marx, *Grundrisse*, 421n.

16. Marx, *Theories of Surplus Value*, 2:505, 531.

17. Marx, *Capital*, 3:614; Marx, *Capital*, 2:391.

18. Marx, *Capital*, 2:391n.

19. Marx, *Capital*, 1:580.

20. Marx, *Theories of Surplus Value*, 2:497.

21. Marx, *Capital*, 3:357.

22. Marx, *Theories of Surplus Value*, 2:497n.

23. Marx, *Grundrisse*, 446.

24. Karl Marx, *Economic Manuscript of 1861–63* (Conclusion) in Marx and Engels, *Collected Works*, vol. 34 (New York: International Publishers 1994), 104.

25. Marx, *Capital*, 3:368.

26. Marx, *Economic Manuscripts of 1861–63* (Conclusion), 104–5.

27. Marx, *Theories of Surplus Value*, 3:447. Note also Marx's comment about McCulloch giving "vent to a veritable jeremiad about the fall in the rate of profit" (186).

28. Hegel, *Science of Logic*, 2:134–35.

29. Lenin, *Philosophical Notebooks*, 150–51.

30. Karl Marx, *Economic and Philosophical Manuscripts of 1844*, in Marx and Engels, *Collected Works*, vol. 3, 270–71.

31. Marx, *Capital*, 3:318.

32. Marx's theoretical exposition of relative surplus value is questioned in Part III of this book.

33. Marx, *Grundrisse*, 773, 771.

34. Marx, *Grundrisse*, 770.

35. Karl Marx, *Economic Manuscripts of 1861–63 (Continuation)*, in Marx and Engels, *Collected Works*, vol. 33 (New York: International Publishers, 1991), 26–29.

36. Ibid., 33–34.

37. Marx, *Capital*, 3:333, 336.

38. *Capital* immediately added that "in practice, however, the rate of profit will fall in the long run." This statement was inserted not by Marx but by Engels. Marx, *Capital*, 3:337; Fred Moseley, "Introduction" to *Marx's Economic Manuscripts of 1864–5* (Boston: Brill, 2016), 20.

39. Marx, *Capital*, 3:346.

40. Marx, *Capital*, 3:333, 368.
41. Marx, *Capital*, 3:201, 203–4; Marx, *Theories of Surplus Value*, 2:28.
42. Marx, *Theories of Surplus Value*, 3: 368.
43. Marx, *Capital*, 3:901.
44. Marx, *Grundrisse*, 754, 752; *Theories of Surplus Value*,2:18.
45. Marx, *Economic Manuscripts of 1861–63 (Continuation)*, 34.
46. Marx, *Capital*, 3:213–14.
47. Marx, *Theories of Surplus Value*, 2:516–17.
48. Marx, *Capital*, 1:579.
49. Marx, *Capital*, 3:201.
50. Marx, *Capital*, 3:362.
51. Marx, *Capital*, 3:214.
52. Marx, *Grundrisse*, 409.
53. Levins and Lewontin, *The Dialectical Biologist*, 280.
54. Marx, *Capital*, 1:899.
55. Lukács, *History and Class Consciousness*, 244.
56. Marx, *Capital*, 3:911.
57. Lebowitz, *The Socialist Imperative*, chap. 1.
58. Marx, *Capital*, 1:638.
59. Marx, *Capital*, 3:949.
60. Marx, *Capital*, 1:381.
61. Levins and Lewontin, *The Dialectical Biologist*, 282. See the discussion in chapter 2 of this book.

5. Never Forget the Second Part

1. Hegel, *Phenomenology*, 81.
2. Hegel, *Science of Logic*, vol. 1: Introduction, 64–66.
3. Hegel, *Phenomenology*, 238–39, 242.
4. Lenin, *Philosophical Notebooks*, 146–47; Ludwig Feuerbach, *Preliminary Theses on the Reform of Philosophy* (1842), in *The Fiery Brook: Selected Writings of Ludwig Feuerbach* (New York: Anchor Books, 1972), 171.
5. Karl Marx, *Contribution to the Critique of Hegel's Philosophy of Law*, in Marx and Engels, *Collected Works*, vol. 3 (New York: International Publishers, 1975), 11, 40.
6. Karl Marx, 1844, 328.
7. Ibid., 329, 332–33, 342.
8. For example, they note that "English and French workers have formed associations in which they exchange opinions not only on their immediate needs as workers, but on their needs as human beings." Further, those workers are conscious of the "power which arises from their cooperation" and "know that property, capital, money, wage-

labour and the like" will not be abolished by "pure thinking" but only "in a practical, objective way." Marx and Engels, *The Holy Family*, in Marx and Engels, *Collected Works*, vol. 4 (New York: International Publishers, 1975), 52–53.

9.   Marx and Engels, *German Ideology*, in Marx and Engels, *Collected Works*, vol. 5 (New York: International Publishers, 1976), 36.

10. Ibid., 53.

11. Ibid., 323.

12. Ibid., 214.

13. Marx, *Theses on Feuerbach*, in Marx and Engels, *Collected Works*, vol. 5 (New York: International Publishers, 1976), 3.

14. Marx, 1844 mss, 329, 332–33, 342.

15. Marx, *Theses on Feuerbach*, 4.

16. We may not grasp the centrality of this point because the third thesis in Engels's widely read edit of Marx's *Theses on Feuerbach* reads: "The coincidence of the changing of circumstances and of human activity can be conceived and rationally understood only as revolutionising practice." That is, it strangely deletes "or self-change" from Marx's text. Marx and Engels, *Collected Works*, vol. 5 (New York: International Publishers, 1976), 7.

17. Marx, *Grundrisse*, 494.

18. Marx, *Capital,* 1:283.

19. Marx, *Capital*, 1:548, 643, 799.

20. Marx, *Capital*, vol. 1, 772.

21. Karl Marx, *Capital*, 3:178; Marx, *Capital,* 1:447.

22. Marx, *Grundrisse*, 488, 541, 708.

23. Marx, *Grundrisse*, 158–59.

24. Karl Marx, *Critique of the Gotha Programme*, in Marx and Engels, *Selected Works*, vol. 2 (Moscow: Foreign Languages Press, 1962), 24.

25. Karl Marx, "Revelations Concerning the Communist Trial in Cologne," in Marx and Engels, *Collected Works,* vol. 11 (New York: International Publishers, 1979), 403.

26. Marx, *The Civil War in France*, in Marx and Engels, *On the Paris Commune* (Moscow: Progress Publishers, 1971), 76.

27. Marx, *Poverty of Philosophy*, 211.

28. Marx, *Capital,* 1:902–4.

29. Marx to Schweitzer, 1 October 13, 1868, in Marx and Engels, *Collected Works,* vol. 43 (New York: International Publishers, 1988), 133–34. Emphasis in the original.

30. Friedrich Engels, "The Ten Hours' Question," in Marx and Engels, *Collected Works*, vol. 10 ((New York: International Publishers, 1978), 275.

31. Marx, *Theories of Surplus Value*, 2:329; Lebowitz, *Beyond* Capital, 185.
32. Marx, *Capital*, 1:412.
33. Lucien Sève, *Man in Marxist Theory and the Psychology of Personality* (Sussex: Harvester Press, 1978), 304.
34. Ibid., 313.
35. Lebowitz, *Beyond* Capital, 142.
36. In chapter 8 of *Beyond* Capital, "The One-Sidedness of Wage-Labour," I posited patriarchy as rooted in a slave relation within the household with the result that male and female wage-laborers are produced differently (144–54).
37. I stressed this point, noting the problem of education that could not be utilized, in a talk I presented at the University of Havana in November 2016, subsequently published as Michael A. Lebowitz, "Protagonism and Productivity" in *Monthly Review* 69/6 (November 2017).
38. Just as Marx spoke metaphorically of the renewal of the worker in his free time as "the production of *fixed capital*, this fixed capital being man himself," one might speak of a tendency for moral depreciation of human capacity that has been built up, all other things equal, if it is not used. Marx, *Grundrisse*, 711–12.
39. See the discussion of simple, contracted, and expanded reproduction of capacity in Lebowitz, "Protagonism and Productivity,"

6. The Burden of Classical Political Economy

1. Karl Marx, "Russian Policy Against Turkey—Chartism" (1853), in Marx and Engels, *Collected Works*, vol. 12 (New York: International Publishers, 1979), 169.
2. Karl Marx, *Value, Price and Profit*, 148.
3. Karl Marx, *Capital*, 1:274.
4. Ibid., 1:660.
5. David Ricardo, *The Principles of Political Economy and Taxation* (London: Dent. Everyman's Library, No. 590, 1969), 260.
6. Karl Marx, "Critical Marginal Notes on the Article by a Prussian," in Marx and Engels, *Collected Works*, vol. 3 (New York: International Publishers, 1975), 192.
7. Karl Marx, 1844 *Manuscripts*, 283–84.
8. Karl Marx, *Poverty of Philosophy*, 125.
9. Marx, *Capital*, 1:275–76, 655.
10. Karl Marx, *Economic Manuscripts of 1861–63*, in Marx and Engels, *Collected Works*, vol. 30 (New York: International Publishers, 1988), 45–6.
11. See the discussion of the Ricardian Default in Michael A. Lebowitz, "Trapped Inside the Box? Five Questions for Ben Fine," *Historical Materialism*, 18/1 (March 2010).

12. Marx, *Capital,* 1:276, 656.

13. Ibid., 436–37.

14. Karl Marx, *Theories of Surplus Value*, vol. 1 (Moscow: Foreign Languages Publishing House, n.d.), 44–45, 68, 296. See the discussion of Marx's assumption and his intention to remove it in Lebowitz, *Beyond* Capital.

15. Karl Marx, *Capital,* vol. 3, 289–90.

16. Karl Marx, *Capital,* vol. 2, 414.

17. Marx, *Capital,* 1:769.

18. Marx, *Capital,* 1:659.

19. Karl Marx, *Economic Manuscripts of 1861–63* (Conclusion), 65–66.

20. Marx and Engels, *Collected Works*, vol. 40 (New York: International Publishers, 1983), 298.

21. Karl Marx, *Grundrisse*, 817. By this "minimum," Marx explained, he meant "not the extreme limit of physical necessity but the average daily wage over e.g. one year." Marx, *Economic Manuscripts of 1861–63,* 52.

22. Karl Marx, *Economic Manuscripts of 1861–63*, 44–45.

23. Marx, *Economic Manuscripts of 1861–63* (Conclusion), 23.

24. Marx, *Capital,* 1:1068–9.

25. Ibid., 1:683. See also "The Missing Book on Wage–Labour," in Lebowitz, *Beyond* Capital, chap. 3.

26. Marx, *Economic Manuscripts of 1861–63*, 44–47.

27. See the discussion of the second moment of production and the household sphere in in Lebowitz, *Beyond* Capital.

28. Marx, *Capital,* 3:289–90.

29. Marx, *Capital,* 1:769. Marx, *Grundrisse*: 287. In such cases, the *quality* of the workers increases, in contrast to the case where real wages are driven down, tending to "degrade" the worker "to the level of the Irish, the level of wage–labour where the most animal minimum of needs and subsistence appears to him as the sole object and purpose of his exchange with capital" (Marx, *Grundrisse*: 285–7). See Lebowitz, *Beyond* Capital, "One–Sided Marxism," chap. 7.

30. Marx, *Capital,* 1:1033.

7. Capital's Need to Separate Workers

1. Marx, *Capital,* vol. 1, 424, 1026.

2. Ibid., 344.

3. Ibid., 899–901, 903–4.

4. For an extended discussion, see chapter 11, "What Is Competition?" in Lebowitz, *Following Marx*.

5. Marx, *Capital,* 1:433.

6. Ibid., 436; Marx, *Grundrisse*, 657, 414.

7.   Marx, *Grundrisse*, 752; Marx, *Capital*, 1: 433.

8.   Karl Marx, "Address of the General Council of the International Working Men's Association to the Members and Associated Societies," July 9, 1867, *Minutes of the General Council of the First International, 1866–68* (Moscow: Progress Publishers, n.d.), 137.

9.   Marx, *Capital*, 1:689, 789, 793.

10. Ibid., 1:697.

11. Ibid., 1:695.

12. Marx, *Grundrisse*, 651.

13. Marx, *Grundrisse*, 414, 657, 752.

14. Marx, *Capital*, vol. 3, 338. See "The Fallacy of Everyday Notions," in Lebowitz, *Following Marx*, chap. 3.

15. Karl Marx, "Inaugural Address of the Working Men's International Association," in Marx and Engels, *Collected Works*, vol. 20 (New York: International Publishers,1985; Levins and Lewontin, *The Dialectical Biologist*, 11. See Lebowitz, *Beyond* Capital, "The Political Economy of Wage–Labour," chap. 4.

16. Marx, *Capital*, 1:280.

17. Ibid., 1:899.

18. Ibid., 1:793, 899.

19. Marx, "Inaugural Address," 11.

20. Marx, *Capital*, 1:171.

21. Marx, *Grundrisse*, 597; Marx, *Theories of Surplus Value*, Vol. 3:312.

22. Engels, "The Wages System, " in W. O. Henderson, ed., *Engels: Selected Writings* (London: Penguin, 1967), 102.

23. Marx, *Value, Price and Profit*, in Marx and Engels, *Collected Works*, vol. 20; Levins and Lewontin, *The Dialectical Biologist*, 148–49, 14; Marx, "Provisional Rules of the Association," in Marx and Engels, *Collected Works*, Vol. 20.

24. Marx, *Capital*, 1:793.

25. Ibid.,1:902–4.

26. Lebowitz, *Beyond* Capital, 159–60.

27. Marx, *Capital*, 1:591.

28. David R. Roediger, *Class, Race, and Marxism* (New York: Verso, 2017), 25–26. Roediger criticizes the distinction that David Harvey "makes between capital, whose logic is said to exclude racial divisions, and capitalism."

29. Levins and Lewontin, *The Dialectical Biologist*, 108.

30. Lewontin and Levins, *Biology Under the Influence*, 150–51.

31. Marx, *Capital*, 1:799. See "Good-bye to Vanguard Marxism," chap. 8 in Michael A. Lebowitz, *The Contradictions of "Real Socialism": The Conductor and the Conducted* (New York: Monthly Review Press, 2012).

32. The political economy of the working class "stresses the combination of labour as the source of social productivity and the separation of workers as the condition for their exploitation." Lebowitz, *Beyond* Capital: 87.
33. Marx, *Capital*, 1:793–94.

8. Beyond Atomism

1. Frederick Engels, "The Constitutional Question in Germany" (1847), in Marx and Engels, *Collected Works*, vol. 6 (New York, International Publishers, 1976), 83–84.
2. Ibid.
3. For example, see Elinor Ostrom, *Governing the Commons: The Evolution of Institutions for Collective Action* (Cambridge: Cambridge University Press, 1990); and Daniel W. Bromley, ed., *Making the Commons Work: Theory, Practice, Policy* (San Francisco: ICS Press, 1992).
4. Marx, *Capital*, 3:754n. See Lebowitz, *The Socialist Imperative*, 22–26, 32–34, esp. "Expanding the Commons," 146–48.
5. Ostrom, *Governing the Commons*, 88.
6. Lebowitz, *The Socialist Alternative*, 66–68; Lebowitz, *The Socialist Imperative*, 26–27. See also Marx, *Grundrisse*, 158, 171–72.
7. E. P. Thompson, "The Moral Economy of the English Crowd in the Eighteenth Century," *Past and Present* 50 (1971).
8. James C. Scott, *The Moral Economy of the Peasant: Rebellion and Subsistence in Southeast Asia* (New Haven: Yale University Press, 1976), 4–5, 7.
9. Lebowitz, *The Socialist Imperative*, chap. 9.
10. Thompson, "The Moral Economy of the English Crowd in the Eighteenth Century," 129.
11. Marx, *Value, Price and Profit*, 143–45.
12. Ibid., 148–49.
13. Daniel Kahneman, Jack L. Knetsch, Richard H. Thaler, "Fairness and the Assumptions of Economics," *Journal of Business*, 59/4 (October 1986).
14. Daniel Kahneman, Jack L. Knetsch, Richard H. Thaler, "Fairness as a Constraint on Profit Seeking: Entitlements in the Market," *American Economic Review* 76/4 (September 1986): 730–31.
15. Kahneman, Knetsch, Thaler, "Fairness and the Assumptions of Economics," S299.
16. Samuel Bowles, *The Moral Economy: Why Good Incentives Are No Substitute for Good Citizens* (New Haven: Yale University Press, 2016).
17. Ibid., 4. Bowles refers to 51 studies, involving 26,000 subjects in 36 countries.
18. Ibid., 5, 9, 98–9.
19. Ibid., 50.

20. Ibid., 5, 9–10.
21. Ibid., 115–18.
22. Ibid., 111.
23. Ibid.; Bowles, *The Moral Economy*, 122. Note that his arguments about the corrosive effects of markets and material incentives upon people are not specific to capitalism but would apply as well to market socialism and, in general, to societies trying to build socialism using material incentives.
24. Ibid., 150.
25. Ibid., 221.
26. See the discussion of separated producers in chapter 3, "The Solidarian Society," in Lebowitz, *The Socialist Alternative*.
27. Marx, *Capital*, 1:280.
28. Only in capitalism does everything have a price, including, Marx mocked, "virtue, love, conviction, knowledge, conscience, etc." Karl Marx, *The Poverty of Philosophy*, 113.
29. Marx, *Grundrisse*, 278, 459–60.
30. In contrast to "communism," designation as "community" highlights relations among people.
31. Marx, *Grundrisse*, 172; Marx, *Capital*, 1:171.
32. Marx, *Grundrisse*, 171–72.
33. Lebowitz, *The Socialist Alternative*, 85–89; Marx, *Grundrisse*, 278.
34. Emily Kawano, *Solidarity Economy: Building an Economy for People & Planet*, https://thenextsystem.org/learn/stories/solidarity-economy-building-economy-people-planet.
35. Marx, "Comments on James Mill," in Marx and Engels, *Collected Works*, vol. 3 (New York: International Publishers, 1975), 227–28; Karl Marx, *Economic and Philosophical Manuscripts of 1844*, 302, 304.
36. Lebowitz, *The Socialist Alternative*, 78–81; Marx, *Grundrisse*, 158–59.
37. Marx, *The Poverty of Philosophy*; 113. Note that Bowles cites this discussion in *The Moral Economy*, 113.
38. Marx's *Critique of the Gotha Programme* should be understood in this context. See chapter 2, "Understanding the Critique of the Gotha Programme," in Lebowitz, *The Socialist Imperative*.

9. Between Organic Systems

1. Marx, *Grundrisse*, 278.
2. Ibid.
3. Ibid., 459–60.
4. For example, in capitalism as an organic system, capital does not need to divide workers because they already are divided; they are atomistic individuals competing with one another.

5. George Wilhelm Friedrich Hegel, *The Philosophy of History* (New York: Dover Publications, 1956), 26.

6. Lebowitz, *The Socialist Alternative*; Lebowitz, *The Contradictions of "Real" Socialism.*

7. Evgeny Preobrazhensky, *The New Economics* (Oxford: Clarendon Press, 1965), 77.

8. Ibid., 102–3, 147–48, 62–65.

9. Ibid., 64.

10. Ibid., 176–77.

11. Evgeny Preobrazhensky, *"The Crisis of Soviet Industrialization": Selected Essays* (White Plains, NY: M. E. Sharpe, 1979), 68.

12. Preobrazhensky, *The New Economics*, 53.

13. Ibid., 176–77.

14. Ibid., 161–62.

15. Ibid., 178.

16. Preobrazhensky, *"The Crisis of Soviet Industrialization,"* 173.

17. A more complex description of relations in that period might identify producer-owned production (within the *mir*, the peasant commune), money-capital, socialism, and state capitalism.

18. Levins and Lewontin, *The Dialectical Biologist*, 280.

19. Marx, *Capital*, 1:931.

20. Marx, *Capital*, 1:874.

21. Marx, *Capital*, 1:927.

22. Jairus Banaji, *Theory as History: Essays on Modes of Production and Exploitation* (Chicago: Haymarket Books, 2011).

23. Marx, *Capital*, 1:382.

24. Lebowitz, *The Socialist Alternative*, 96–98. Those methods are not required in capitalism as an organic system.

25. Marx, *Capital*, 1:899, 904–5.

26. Karl Marx, *Economic Manuscripts of 1861–63*, 116; Lebowitz, *Beyond Capital*, 124–30.

27. Marx, *Capital*, 1:716, 718.

28. Italics added. Here is the point that Marx considered so central that he made it in the closing chapter of Volume 1 of *Capital*. Indeed, this quotation is from the closing sentence of the volume!

29. Banaji, *Theory as History*.

30. Ibid., 11.

31. Ibid., 8, 61.

32. Review chapter 3 to see how consistent "pseudo-Marx" is in describing wage-labor as the premise and result of capitalism. Marx, *Capital*, 1:325, 723–24, 874; Marx, *Capital*, vol 3, 927.

33. Banaji, *Theory as History*, 11, 9, 41.

34. Ibid., 41.
35. Ibid., 69–70, 93, 94–96.
36. Ibid., 45, 357–58.
37. Ibid., 273; Preobrazhensky, *The New Economics*, 77.
38. Note that the systems in struggle are not necessarily limited to two. In "Contested Reproduction and the Contradictions of Socialism" (chapter 4 of *The Socialist Imperative*), I described the interaction of three logics in Yugoslav Self-Management: the logic of the vanguard, the logic of capital, and the logic of the working class.
39. Lewontin and Levins, *Biology Under the Influence*, 196–98.

10. How to Find a Path to Community

1. Wassily Leontiev, *Essays in Economics: Theories and Theorizing* (New York: Oxford University Press, 1966), 14.
2. Ibid., 15.
3. Ibid.,16.
4. Ollman, *Dance of the Dialectic*, 163.
5. Ibid., 119.
6. Lewontin and Levin, *Biology Under the Influence*, 279.
7. Marx, *Grundrisse*, 460–61.
8. Marx and Engels, *Communist Manifesto*, in Marx and Engels, *Collected Works*, vol. 6 (New York: International Publishers, 1976), 495.
9. Ibid., 504.
10. Lebowitz, "Understanding the *Critique of the Gotha Programme*," chapter 2 in *The Socialist Imperative*.
11. Lebowitz, *The Contradictions of "Real Socialism*," 135–38; see also chap. 5 in that book, "The Conductor and the Battle of Ideas in the Soviet Union."
12. Karl Marx, *The Civil War in France*, in Marx and Engels, *On the Paris Commune* (Moscow: Progress Publishers, 1971), 68–73.
13. Karl Marx, "First Outline of *The Civil War in France*," in Marx and Engels, *On the Paris Commune*, 155–56.
14. Ibid., 154–55.
15. Marx, *Civil War in France*, 75.
16. Lebowitz, *The Contradictions of "Real Socialism."*
17. Ibid., 63–65.
18. See, in particular, "The Nature and Reproduction of Vanguard Relations of Production," chapter 3 in Lebowitz, *The Contradictions of "Real Socialism."*
19. I am describing the vanguard party here as generally understood in its "purity," not how it may have been transformed by its inner logic and interactions with other relations (nor how it could be different). See Lebowitz, *The Contradictions of "Real Socialism*," for a full analysis.

20. "Contested Reproduction and the Contradictions of Socialism," in Lebowitz, *The Socialist Imperative.*

21. This scenario is at the core of the nomenklatura and the effort by some to display exemplary behavior with respect to carrying out the line on "real socialism."

22. Lebowitz, *The Contradictions of "Real Socialism,"* 72–74.

23. See the discussion in Lebowitz, *The Socialist Alternative*, 48–50.

11. Taking a Path to Community

1. Marx and Engels, *Communist Manifesto*, 506.

2. Marx, *Grundrisse*, 172; Marx, *Capital,* 1:171.

3. Marx, *Capital*, 3:911, 916.

4. Marx, *Capital*, 1:635–36.

5. Marx, *Capital*, 3:754n.

6. Marx, *Capital*, 3:911.

7. Marx, *Capital*, 3:949.

8. "How did we win?" is a question posed in strategic workshops by the U.S. socialist group LeftRoots, https://leftroots.net/.

9. Levins and Lewontin, *The Dialectical Biologist*, 282.

10. A Marxist who believes that the struggle against capital and for community really is only to be found in the capitalist workplace reflects the one-sided perspective of capital, for which only the direct challenges initiated by workers to the expanded reproduction of capital matter.

11. Engels, "The Constitutional Question. . . ."

12. A question I posed to Venezuelan workers in a 2005 talk about worker management was: "In a system of worker self-management, who looks after the interests of the working class as a whole?" See "Seven Difficult Questions," in Lebowitz, *Build It Now*, and my discussion of Marx's views of the cooperative factories of his time in *Beyond* Capital, 88–89.

13. Lebowitz, *Beyond* Capital, 90–98, 111–12.

14. Ibid., 188–89.

15. Marx, "Inaugural Address of the Working Men's International Association," 11–12; Lebowitz, *Beyond* Capital, 88–89.

16. See Michael A, Lebowitz, "Seven Difficult Questions," in *Build It Now*, chap. 6. See also Lebowitz, *The Socialist Alternative*, chap. 3; and "Contested Reproduction and the Contradictions of Socialism," in Lebowitz, *The Socialist Imperative*, chap. 4.

17. Sharryn Kasmir, *The Myth of Mondragon: Cooperatives, Politics, and Working-Class Life in a Basque Town* (Albany: State University of New York Press, 1996), 195–99.

18. Robert Michels, *Political Parties: A Sociological Study of the Oligarchic*

Tendencies of Modern Democracy (New York: Collier Books, 1962), 70–77, 87–91, 350–53.

19. Michael A. Lebowitz, "The Nature and Reproduction of Vanguard Relations of Production," in *The Contradictions of "Real Socialism,"* chap. 3.

20. Paulo Freire, *Pedagogy of the Oppressed*, 72–73.

21. Lebowitz, *Contradictions of "Real Socialism"*; Lebowitz, *The Socialist Imperative*, chapter 4, "Contested Reproduction and the Contradictions of Socialism."

12. The Political Instrument We Need

1. Lazy Leninists doubtless feel that authoritative quotes and citations from Lenin are sufficient to make the point.

2. Murray Bookchin, *The Next Revolution: Popular Assemblies and the Promise of Direct Democracy* (New York: Verso, 2015), 180–81. Bookchin's influence on developments in Rojava via Abdullah Öcalan provides a reason to look back at him for those unfamiliar with his work. See Debbie Bookchin, "How My Father's Ideas Helped the Kurds Create a New Democracy," https://www.nybooks.com/daily/2018/06/15/how-my-fathers-ideas-helped-the-kurds-create-a-new-democracy/nybooks.com.

3. Marta Harnecker, *A World to Build: New Paths toward Twenty-First Century Socialism* (New York: Monthly Review Press, 2015), 165–66.

4. Marta Harnecker, "Ideas for the Struggle," 2016, http://www.oldandnewproject.net/Essays/Harnecker_Ideas.html.

5. Marx to Schweitzer, 13 October 1868, in Marx and Engels, *Collected Works*, vol. 43 (New York: International Publishers, 1988), 133–34. Emphasis in the original.

6. This perspective clearly accepts the premise in Article 62 of the Bolivarian Constitution that the protagonism of people is "the necessary way of achieving the involvement to ensure their complete development, both individual and collective." Harnecker, *A World to Build*, 179.

7. Lucien Sève, *Man in Marxist Theory and the Psychology of Personality*, 313.

8. Harnecker, *A World to Build*, 72. See the extended development of this perspective with respect to communities in Marta Harnecker and José Bartolomé, *Planning from Below: A Decentralized Participatory Planning Proposal* (New York: Monthly Review Press, 2019).

9. Harnecker, *A World to Build*, 154.

10. Harnecker and Bartolomé, *Planning from Below*, 18, 25.

11. Bookchin, *The Next Revolution*, 158 and passim.

12. Lebowitz, *The Socialist Imperative*: chap. 10, 201, 218–199. Though there

are obvious parallels with respect to the importance of "walking on two legs," Bookchin's horizon is the municipality; he rejects Marxism for its emphasis on the working class and accordingly also rejects the idea of workers as such making decisions. Reflecting his anarchist history, further, he refuses to call what Chávez described as these "cells of a new socialist state" a state.

13. Vivek Chibber, "Our Path to Power, " *Jacobin*, December 5, 2017.

14. To provide theoretical justification for what might otherwise be seen as opportunism or a transitory tactic, the pre-renegade Kautsky has been exhumed (especially in *Jacobin* magazine) in order to marshal theoretical authority for the electoral struggle. True, Kautsky was an advocate of electoralism by a separate working-class party rather than supporting a party of capital but it might be argued that this simply reflects the vast difference between the current conjuncture and the one in which Kautsky wrote *The Road to Power*.

15. Of course, discontent with change does not necessarily look forward to a future path. Characteristic of moral economy is a tendency to look backward to real or imagined (and idealized) previous states of society, and this very circumstance is fertile ground for the Far Right, fertile ground for the emergence of scapegoating (for example, of immigrants), demagoguery, and national chauvinism.

16. Lebowitz, *Build It Now*, chap. 2.

17. In *"Social Democracy or Revolutionary Democracy: Syriza and Us,"* https://socialistproject.ca/2015 /08/b1149/, I argued: "There are always choices. We can take the path of 'defeats without glory' (Badiou) characteristic of social democracy or we can move in the direction of the revolutionary democracy that builds the capacities of the working class. At the core of the latter is that it embraces the centrality of the concept of revolutionary practice—'the coincidence of the changing of circumstances and human activity or self–change.'"

18. See the discussion of the old state and the new state in Michael Lebowitz, *Building Socialism for the 21st Century: The Logic of the State*, the Fourth Annual Nicos Poulantzas Memorial Lecture, 8 December 2010 (published by the Poulantzas Institute in 2011). This talk appeared in an expanded version as "The State and the Future of Socialism" in the *Socialist Register 2013* and is included as chapter 10 of *The Socialist Imperative*.

19. Lebowitz, *Contradictions of "Real Socialism,"* 69.

20. Harnecker, "Ideas for the Struggle."

21. Freire, *Pedagogy of the Oppressed*, 71–73.

22. Ibid., 60.

23. Ibid., 65, 67.

24. Idea #1, Harnecker, "Ideas for the Struggle."
25. Idea #3, "To be at the service of popular movements, not to displace them." Ibid.
26. Ibid.
27. Marx and Engels, *The Communist Manifesto*, 518.
28. Harnecker, "Ideas for the Struggle."
29. Lebowitz, *The Socialist Alternative*, 160–62.
30. Lewontin and Levins, *Biology Under the Influence*, 150–51, 108.
31. Kawano, *Solidarity Economy: Building an Economy for People & Planet.*
32. Levins and Lewontin, *The Dialectical Biologist*, 282.
33. Lebowitz, *The Socialist Imperative*, 202.
34. Karl Marx to Frederick Engels, 9 April 1863, in Marx and Engels, *Collected Works*, vol. 41 (New York: International Publishers, 1985), 468. Harnecker cites Lenin, too, with respect to the lessons of the February Revolution, that there can be events when "millions and tens of millions of people learn in a week more than they do in a year of ordinary somnolent life." Marta Harnecker, *Rebuilding the Left* (London: Zed Books, 2007), 58.
35. Lewontin and Levins, *Biology Under the Influence*, 77, 182.

Index

abstract surplus value, 97–98
accumulation, 14, 46, 50, 82; feedback from, 98–99; production and, 132; regulation of, 126–27
agriculture, 64–65
analysis, 36, 137, 139
anarchy, 163–64
atomism, 192n4; fairness and, 114–19; individual, 155; of neoclassical economics, 19–28; separation compared to, 163; for working-class, 111–13, 119–22

bad theory, 131
Banaji, Jairus, 129, 131–35
banking concept of education, 171–72
Bartolomé, José, 165–66
Bastiat, Frédéric, 25–26
behavioral economics, 115
Bolivia, 196n6
Bookchin, Murray, 163–64, 166, 196n12

boom periods, 66
bourgeois system, 43, 47, 53, 120, 140–43
Bowles, Sam, 116–19, 122

Callinicos, Alex, 14–16
capacity, 82–83
capital: *see specific topics*
Capital (Marx), 11–15, 54, 73, 78, 81; class in, 58; history in, 138–39; production in, 37, 44, 56–57; reproduction in, 43–44; surplus value in, 87; systems in, 28; working-class in, 52
capitalism: *see specific topics*
capital-relation, 46
Cartesian reductionism, 29
Castoriadis, Cornelius, 11–12
causality, 33
change, 197n15; crisis and, 178–79, 184n4; from feedback, 35; for individuals, 36; in markets, 115–16; for Marx, 57, 77–78; in Marxism, 106; observation

of, 45; in organic systems, 133–36; potential of, 140–41; self-change, 80–81; in society, 172–73; spontaneity in, 163–64; in working-class, 76, 167–68, 177

Chavez, Hugo, 121

Chibber, Vivek, 167

China, 133–34

choice, 23–26, 186n8, 197n17

circulation, 49–50, 55–57

Clark, John Bates, 24–25

class, 14, 23, 52, 58, 75; exploitation of, 105; ruling, 76, 104, 144–45; struggle, 12–13, 15; war, 15, 81–82; see also working-class

classical political economy: commodities in, 85–86; for Marx, 97; for Ricardo, 87–88; social relations in, 98; surplus value in, 88–92; wage-laborers in, 92–95

classification, 133–36

cognition, 36–37

Cohen, G. A., 27

collective capital, 104

collective labor, 104

colonization, 130–31

commercial capitalism, 133

commodities: in bourgeois system, 120; circulation of, 56–57; in classical political economy, 85–86; economics of, 56, 92–93; exploitation and, 49; labor-power as, 12, 48, 120; for Marx, 55, 120–21; metamorphosis of, 93; raw material for, 64; surplus value and, 44–45; transactions with, 54–55; wage-laborers and, 47–48

communal society: history of, 152–54; ideology of, 157–60; struggle for, 154–56; systems for, 150–52

communism, 142–46; see also real socialism

Communist Manifesto (Marx and Engels), 140–41

community: see specific topics

competition, 99–100, 111, 184n20

The Condition of the Working Class in England (Engels), 75

consumerism, 20–21, 51, 56–57, 133

contemplative materialism, 76

contested reproduction, 125–28, 131–34, 160, 162–63, 177–79

contradiction, 33–34, 38–39, 56–59, 67, 105, 140

Contribution to the Critique of Hegel's Philosophy of Law (Feuerbach), 74

crashes, 58

criminals, 20

crisis, 54–58, 140, 184n4; change after, 178–79, 184n4; of Earth system, 68–70, 175–79; in economics, 67–68, 169–70; in profit, 59–67

Critique of the Gotha Programme (Marx), 79–80, 142

currency, 26

decentralization, 165–66

deduction, 21–22, 36, 144–45

dehumanization, 86

democratic centralism, 147–48

dialectic thinking, 29–30; equilibrium and, 33–34, 67–68; interdependency and, 31; negativity in, 37; parts for, 32–33;

struggle and, 82; teleology and, 139; "Why Dialectics?," 138
The Dialectical Biologist (Levins and Lewontin), 29
directionality, 138
distribution, 144
The Distribution of Wealth (Clark), 24–25
dynamic systems, 137–38

Earth system, 68–70, 175–79
Economic Manuscripts (Marx), 62–63
economics: behavioral, 115; of boom periods, 66; of bourgeois system, 47; of commodities, 56, 92–93; contradiction in, 67; of crashes, 58; crisis in, 67–68, 169–70; economists, 21–22; of equilibrium, 20–21; experimental, 114–19; of markets, 101; of money, 92–95; neoclassical, 19–28, 113; political economy, 55, 59–60; *Principles of Political Economy*, 85–86; of supply-and-demand law, 104; theory and, 25–26
education, 26
egalitarianism, 159
employment, 22–23, 129–30, 146
Engels, Friedrich, 33; atomism for, 111; Marx and, 75–77, 90, 157, 187n16; self-change for, 80–81; separation for, 155; struggle for, 85; trade unions for, 103
equal rights, 15
equilibrium: dialectic thinking and, 33–34, 67–68; economics of, 20–21; feedback for, 114, 135; production and, 57–58, 63;

surplus value and, 55–56; for working-class, 70
exchange, 24, 48, 55
experimental economics, 114–19
exploitation: of class, 105; commodities and, 49; fairness and, 114–15; production and, 106, 131–32; reproduction and, 52–53, 134; of workers, 47, 60, 154–55
expropriation, 130–31
externalities, 26–27

fairness, 113–19, 146, 157
fallacy of composition, 26
falling rate of profit (FROP), 59–60, 62–63, 65, 67
families, 22–23, 75
feedback: from accumulation, 98–99; change from, 35; for equilibrium, 114, 135; non-reproduction and, 130; productivity and, 62; reductionism and, 34; for systems, 61, 63, 178; wages and, 98; workers and, 68–70
feudalism, 133, 139–40
Feurbach, Ludwig, 74, 77
Fine, Ben, 13–14, 16
First International, 103, 112
fixed capital, 66, 188n38
Foster, John Bellamy, 68
Freire, Paolo, 148, 159, 171–72

Galbraith, John Kenneth, 25
General Council (First International), 112
German Ideology (Engels and Marx), 75–77
Gorbachev, Mikhail, 143
Greece, 168–69

Grundrisse (Marx), 12, 36, 55–56, 62, 78, 90–91

Harnecker, Marta, 164–66, 172–73
Harvey, David, 190n28
Hegel, Georg Wilhelm Friedrich, 12–13, 29–31, 35–37; causality for, 33; history for, 124; Marx and, 161–63; revolutionary practice and, 73–78; the whole for, 176; *see also specific works*
hierarchies, 145, 147–48, 157–60
history: in *Capital*, 138–39; colonization, 130–31; of commercial capitalism, 133; of communal society, 152–54; for Hegel, 124; historical materialism, 131–32; of human-activity, 77–78; Latin America, 171–72; of markets, 114; for Marx, 151–52; of production, 193n17; of property, 113; of systems, 46–47, 137–46; of USSR, 126–27; of wage-laborers, 124–25; "When Should History Be Written Backwards?," 137
The Holy Family (Marx and Engels), 75
homeostasis, 135
homo economicus, 115–17, 177
homo solidaricus, 121–22, 150–52, 154, 157, 177
horizontalism, 159
households, 184n18
human-activity, 9, 77–79, 116–17

the Idea, 74–75
idealism, 74, 77
"Ideas for the Struggle" (Harnecker), 173–75
ideology, 96–97, 152–53, 157–60

immanent law, 126, 131
incentives, 117–22
income taxes, 23
individuals: activity of, 121; change for, 36; choice for, 25–26; health of, 22; individual atomism, 155; markets and, 28; for Marx, 30, 79; rational choice of, 20, 23–24, 26–27; reputation of, 113; self-interest of, 19–20; society and, 24, 27–28, 142; struggle of, 156; systems for, 56; wage-laborers as, 100–101, 189n29; workers and, 100
industry, 64–65
interconnection, 36, 101–2
interdependency, 26–28, 31–32
internal relations, 55–56
interpenetration, 32
investments, 55
"Invisible Hand" theory, 25

Japan, 46

Kagarlitsky, Boris, 146
Kasmir, Sharryn, 158
Kautsky, Karl, 197n14
Keynes, John Maynard, 26
knowledge, 35–39, 148

labor: capacity, 90; collective, 104; concepts of, 75; in *Grundrisse*, 78; hierarchies in, 145; machinery for, 99; for Marx, 64–65; nature and, 68–70; price of, 100; production and, 79, 120–21; productivity from, 52, 57, 62–64; regulation and, 57; for Ricardo, 63; standard of necessity for, 97–98; surplus value from, 57; wages and, 48–49; *see also* wage-laborers

labor-power: as commodities, 12, 48, 120; money for, 47; in organic systems, 61; production of, 93; property and, 143; value of, 63, 86–87, 90–91; for wage-laborers, 111–12; for workers, 49, 52, 81, 85, 111–12

laissez-faire policy, 23

Latin America, 171–72

law: concepts of, 60; for human-activity, 116–17; immanent, 126, 131; law of value, 126–27; natural, 80, 140, 150–51; in neoclassical economics, 113; in New York, 81; for regulation, 15; supply-and-demand, 99–102, 104, 120

Lefebvre, Henri, 36

leisure, 20

Lenin, Vladmir, 30–33, 36–38, 74, 196n1, 198n34

Leontiev, Wassily, 137–38

Levins, Richard, 29–31, 33–35, 38–39; change for, 179; contradictions for, 105; dialectic thinking for, 67–68; directionality for, 138; Hegel for, 176; history for, 152; opposing forces for, 128; systems for, 178; theory for, 96–97

Lewontin, Richard, 29–31, 34–35, 38–39; change for, 179; contradictions for, 105; dialectic thinking for, 67–68; directionality for, 138; Hegel for, 176; history for, 152; opposing forces for, 128; systems for, 178; theory for, 96–97

Lukács, György, 30, 32, 39, 68, 141

machinery, 65–66, 99

markets: change in, 115–16; competition in, 99–100; contested reproduction for, 127; economics of, 101; history of, 114; incentives in, 192n23; individuals and, 28; production for, 48

Marx, Karl, 11–16, 36; analysis by, 139; bourgeois system for, 142–43; change for, 57, 77–78; circulation for, 50, 55–56; classical political economy for, 97; commodities for, 55, 120–21; communism for, 142–44; consumerism for, 51; Engels and, 75–77, 90, 157, 187n16; FROP for, 62; Hegel, 161–63; hierarchies for, 157–58; history for, 151–52; individuals for, 30, 79; labor for, 64–65; methodology of, 91–92; mutual interaction for, 33; natural law for, 80, 151; organic systems for, 43–45; *Phenomenology of Mind* for, 75, 83; production for, 45–47; productivity for, 175; profit for, 60–61, 185n38; rational choice for, 59–60; reproduction for, 45–46; Ricardo and, 85–86; supply-and-demand law for, 120; systems for, 128; theory for, 180n1; universal venality for, 122; value for, 66–67; wages for, 114, 189n21; working-class for, 84–85, 104–5, 178; *see also specific works*

Marxism: change in, 106; concepts in, 39; contradiction in, 33–34; interpenetration in, 32; Marxism-Leninism, 148, 163–64; politics of, 27–28; Ricardian

Default and, 92; struggle in, 195n10; theory of, 45–46, 68–69, 83, 89, 134; working-class in, 196n12

materialism, 74, 76–78, 119–20, 122, 131–32, 192n23

minorities, 173–74

Mondragon (corporation), 158

money: currency, 26; economics of, 92–95; for labor-power, 47; money-capital, 129–30; for reproduction, 49–50; reserves of, 88–89; value of, 94–95

The Moral Economy (Bowles), 116–17

"The Moral Economy of the English Crowd" (Thompson), 114

municipality, 166, 196n12

mutual interaction, 33

natural law, 80, 140, 150–51

nature, 68–70, 176–77

neoclassical economics, 19–28, 113

neoliberal state policies, 22, 167–68

New York, 81

nomenklatura, 195n21

non-neutrality, 105–7

non-reproduction, 54–55, 68, 130

observation, 36–37, 45

old society, 155

Ollman, Bertell, 31–33, 38, 138, 142

opposing forces, 128–30

organic systems: of accumulation, 46; atomism and, 192n4; change in, 133–36; concepts of, 123–28; labor-power in, 61; for Marx,

43–45; one-sidedness in, 131–33; opposing forces in, 128–30; profit in, 63–64; separation of, 121–22; state programs and, 141; theory of, 16, 119, 161–62; value in, 61–62; wage-laborers in, 50–53, 181n4

Ostrom, Elinor, 113, 120

overproduction, 55–59, 66

paradox of thrift, 26

parts, 29–33, 125–26, 162–63

patriarchy, 105, 184n18, 188n36

permanent crises, 59

Phenomenology of Mind (Hegel), 29, 74–75, 77, 83

physiocrats, 88

Planning from Below (Bartolomé), 165–66

policy, 22–23, 77, 79–80, 167–68

political instruments: of contested reproduction, 177–79; revolutionary agency, 163–64; revolutionary pedagogue, 171–75; revolutionary practice, 162, 165–66; theory and, 161–63; traditional models of, 167–71

politics: in *Communist Manifesto*, 140–41; hierarchies in, 159–60; of Marxism, 27–28; political cadres, 173–75; political economy, 55, 59–60, 84–85, 101–3; *Principles of Political Economy*, 85–86; of production, 48; society and, 148; of struggle, 153–54; of working-class, 158, 191n32; *see also* classical political economy

poverty, 23, 80

The Poverty of Philosophy (Marx), 80

Poverty of Theory (Thompson), 11
pre-capitalist systems, 50–51
Preobrazhensky, Evgeny, 126–28, 133, 162–63
Principles of Political Economy (Ricardo), 85–86
production: accumulation and, 132; in *Capital*, 37, 44, 56–57; employment and, 129–30; equilibrium and, 57–58, 63; exploitation and, 106, 131–32; after feudalism, 139–40; history of, 193n17; investments and, 55; labor and, 79, 120–21; of labor-power, 93; for markets, 48; for Marx, 45–47; for materialism, 77–78; organization of, 106; politics of, 48; productive forces, 105–7, 127; property and, 150–51; relations of, 124; separation in, 128–29; as slavery, 94; social, 121; for society, 24–25; standard of necessity and, 89–90; supply-and-demand law for, 102; surplus value from, 14–15; systems for, 123–24; value and, 64–65; by wage-laborers, 44–45; of workers, 51–53; *see also specific topics*
productivity: in agriculture, 64–65; feedback and, 62; from labor, 52, 57, 62–64; for Marx, 175; social, 79; surplus value from, 14–15; wages and, 84; of workers, 61
profit, 16, 59–67, 92, 185n38
proletariat, 68, 141
propaganda, 172
property: concepts of, 152; history of, 113; labor-power and, 143; production and, 150–51; social relations and, 112
protagonism, 165–67, 196n6; human-activity and, 9; paradox of, 156; revolutionary practice and, 159–60; for society, 150; theory of, 174–75
Provisional Rules (First International), 103
punishment, 20, 116–17

racism, 105
rational choice, 20, 23–24, 26–27, 59–60
raw material, 64–67
real socialism, 146–49, 159, 168–69
reciprocal interaction, 32–33
reductionism, 31–32, 34
reference transactions, 116
regulation: of accumulation, 126–27; distribution and, 144; labor and, 57; law for, 15; self-regulation, 35, 67; state programs for, 46; systems and, 34–35
relative surplus value, 61, 97–99
religion, 25
reproduction, 45–46, 93; of capacity, 83; in *Capital*, 43–44; contested, 125–28, 131–34, 160, 162–63, 177–79; exploitation and, 52–53, 134; interconnection of, 101–2; money for, 49–50; non-reproduction, 54–55; subordination for, 162; systems and, 34, 147; theory of, 32–35; the whole and, 32–35, 125–28; workers for, 49
reserves, of money, 88–89
revolutionary agency, 163–64
revolutionary pedagogue, 171–75

revolutionary practice, 73–78, 83, 148–49; choice and, 197n17; politics of, 162, 165–66; protagonism and, 159–60

Ricardian Default, 87–88, 92, 94, 96

Ricardo, David, 59, 63, 65, 85–88

The Road to Power (Kautsky), 197n14

ruling class, 76, 104, 144–45

Say, J. B., 55

Science of Logic (Hegel), 30, 36

second product: revolutionary practice and, 73–78; theory of, 78–81; for workers, 82–83

second-order effects, 27

self-change, 80–81

self-interest, 19–20, 24–25

self-management: theory of, 195n12; in Yugoslavia, 134, 141, 143, 155–56, 158, 194n38

self-regulation, 35, 67

separation: atomism compared to, 163; for Engels, 155; of organic systems, 121–22; in production, 128–29; of workers, 96–98, 102–5

Sève, Lucien, 82, 165

slavery, 94–95, 132, 184n18, 188n36

small spaces, 165–66

Smith, Adam, 24–25, 59

social contract theory, 146–47

social democracy, 167–69

social ownership, 151

society: change in, 172–73; deduction for, 144–45; education for, 26; goals for, 150; individuals and, 24, 27–28, 142; *The Moral Economy* about, 116–17; old, 155; policy and, 77; politics and, 148; production for, 24–25; productive forces of, 127; protagonism for, 150; slavery for, 132; social preferences, 117–19, 122; social production, 121; social productivity, 79; social relations, 44, 48, 51, 98, 112, 184n18; structure of, 125; struggle for, 166; systems and, 45; *Why Good Incentives Are No Substitute for Good Citizens*, 118–19; workers for, 69, 94, 119–22; working-class and, 81, 102

Spain, 158

spontaneity, 163–64

standard of necessity, 89–92, 97–98

stasis: *see* equilibrium

state programs, 23, 46, 104, 141, 144–45, 165–68

Stirner, Max, 76

Stone, Oliver, 25

struggle: for alternatives, 177–78; in *Capital*, 14–15; class, 12–13, 15; for communal society, 154–56; contested reproduction and, 160; dialectic thinking and, 82; for Engels, 85; "Ideas for the Struggle," 173–75; of individuals, 156; in Marxism, 195n10; of minorities, 173–74; politics of, 153–54; poverty and, 80; for real socialism, 168–69; for society, 166; systems in, 194n38; over Ten Hours Bill, 153; wages and, 16, 84; workers and, 103–4, 166; for working-class, 163, 165

subordination, 97–101, 143, 162

supply-and-demand law, 99–102, 104, 120

supremacy, 97–101
surplus value: abstract, 97–98; in *Capital*, 87; from circulation, 50; in classical political economy, 88–92; commodities and, 44–45; equilibrium and, 55–56; from labor, 57; for nature, 176–77; from productivity, 14–15; profit and, 60–62; relative, 61, 97–99; from workers, 49
Syriza party, 168–69
systems: anarchy, 163–64; bourgeois, 43, 47, 53, 120, 142–43; in *Capital*, 28; for communal society, 150–52; dynamic, 137–38; Earth system, 68–70, 175–79; feedback for, 61, 63, 178; hierarchies in, 147–48; history of, 46–47, 137–46; for individuals, 56; interdependency and, 28; for Marx, 128; pre-capitalist, 50–51; for production, 123–24; regulation and, 34–35; reproduction and, 34, 147; society and, 45; in struggle, 194n38; theory, 31; the whole in, 135–36; *see also* organic systems

teleology, 139
Ten Hours Bill, 153
Thompson, E. P., 11–12, 114
totality of thoughts, 37
trade unions, 103
traditional models, of politics, 167–71
traditional standard of life, 114
transactions, 54–55, 116

the ultimatum game, 115
underproduction, 66–67
unemployment, 22–24

Union of Soviet Socialist Republics (USSR), 126–27, 134
universal venality, 122
Unoism, 13
unreconstructed Hegelianism, 12–13
unutilized capacity, 83
use-values, 47–48, 66–67, 89

value, 44–45; of currency, 26; exchange, 48, 55; of labor-power, 63, 86–87, 90–91; law of value, 126–27; for Marx, 66–67; of money, 94–95; in organic systems, 61–62; production and, 64–65; profit and, 16; theory of, 13; use-values, 47–48, 66–67, 89; *see also* surplus value
Value, Price, and Profit (Marx), 16, 103, 114
vanguard party, 147–49, 159, 171, 194n19
Veblen, Thorstin, 19–20
verticalism, 173–74

wage-laborers: in classical political economy, 92–95; commodities and, 47–48; history of, 124–25; as individuals, 100–101, 189n29; labor-power for, 111–12; in organic systems, 50–53, 181n4; production by, 44–45; study of, 91; as workers, 82
wages: in bourgeois system, 53; in *Capital*, 13–14; capital-relation, 46; consumerism and, 21; fairness in, 157; feedback and, 98; in *Grundrisse*, 90–91; labor and, 48–49; for Marx, 114, 189n21; minimum of, 88, 91; productivity and, 84; struggle and, 16, 84;

welfare and, 22–23; for workers, 189n29; for working-class,
47–50
Wakefield, E. G., 130–31
Wall Street (film), 25
welfare, 22–23
Western Europe, 139
"When Should History Be Written
Backwards?" (Leontiev), 137
the whole: classification of, 134–
35; contested reproduction and,
162–63; contradiction and, 105;
for Hegel, 176; knowing, 35–39;
parts and, 29–32; reproduction
and, 32–35, 125–28; in systems, 135–36; theory of, 73–74,
161–62
"Why Dialectics?" (Ollman), 138
*Why Good Incentives Are No
Substitute for Good Citizens*
(Bowles), 118–19
workers: in accumulation, 50;
in *Capital*, 11–12, 54, 78, 81;
choice for, 23–24, 186n8;
competition for, 111, 184n20;
*The Condition of the Working
Class in England*, 75; councils,
156; dehumanization of, 86;
dilemma, 112; equal rights
for, 15; exploitation of, 47,
60, 154–55; expropriation of,
130–31; feedback and, 68–70;
fixed capital for, 188n38; goals

of, 12–13; human-activity
and, 78–79; individuals and,
100; labor-power for, 49, 52,
81, 85, 111–12; leisure for, 20;
policy by, 79–80; production
by, 51–53; productive forces
and, 105–7; productivity of, 61;
for reproduction, 49; second
product for, 82–83; separation
of, 96–98, 102–5; for society, 69,
94, 119–22; struggle and, 103–4,
166; subordination of, 97–101;
supply-and-demand for, 101–2;
surplus value from, 49; as wage-
laborers, 82; wages for, 189n29
working-class: atomism for,
111–13, 119–22; in *Capital*,
52; change in, 76, 167–68, 177;
concepts of, 154–55; division
of, 102–7; equilibrium for, 70;
for Marx, 84–85, 104–5, 178; in
Marxism, 196n12; organization
of, 170; politics of, 158, 191n32;
society and, 81, 102; struggle
for, 163, 165; theory of, 170–71;
wages for, 47–50
A World to Build (Harnecker),
164–65

xenophobia, 105

Yugoslavia, 134, 143, 155–56, 158,
194n38